First World War
and Army of Occupation
War Diary
France, Belgium and Germany

14 DIVISION
Divisional Troops
Divisional Trench Mortar Batteries
24 June 1915 - 29 January 1919

WO95/1888/1

The Naval & Military Press Ltd
www.nmarchive.com
Published in association with The National Archives

Published by

The Naval & Military Press Ltd

Unit 10 Ridgewood Industrial Park,

Uckfield, East Sussex,

TN22 5QE England

Tel: +44 (0) 1825 749494

www.naval-military-press.com

www.nmarchive.com

This diary has been reprinted in facsimile from the original. Any imperfections are inevitably reproduced and the quality may fall short of modern type and cartographic standards.

Contents

Document type	Place/Title	Date From	Date To
Heading	1888/1 14th Division Trench Mortar Batteries		
Heading	14th Division Trench Mortar Batteries Jun 1915-Jan 1919		
Heading	14 Div 29th Trench Hors Batty Vol I 24-30.6.15 Jan 19		
War Diary	I 11 A Ref. 1/40,000	24/06/1915	01/07/1915
Miscellaneous	14th Div 14th T M Batt		
War Diary	Valheureux	02/03/1916	02/03/1916
War Diary	Fosseux	08/03/1916	08/03/1916
War Diary	Dainville	11/03/1916	20/03/1916
Heading	Y 14 Trench M B Vol 1		
War Diary	Valheureux	02/03/1916	08/03/1916
War Diary	Fosseux	09/03/1916	11/03/1916
War Diary	Dainville	11/03/1916	19/03/1916
War Diary	Trenches	20/03/1916	30/03/1916
Heading	Z/14 T M Bty Vol I		
War Diary	Field	01/03/1916	31/03/1916
Miscellaneous	To Officer i/c Hence Records	14/04/1916	14/04/1916
War Diary	Field	01/03/1916	31/03/1916
Heading	Y 14 T M Bty Vol I		
War Diary		01/04/1916	28/04/1916
War Diary	Blangy	01/05/1916	08/05/1916
War Diary	St Sauveur Blaugy &	10/05/1916	10/05/1916
War Diary	St Sauveur	11/05/1916	11/05/1916
War Diary	Blangy	15/05/1916	20/05/1916
War Diary	St. Sauveur	21/05/1916	21/05/1916
War Diary	Blangy	28/05/1916	28/05/1916
War Diary	Ronville	29/05/1916	29/05/1916
War Diary	Field In Front Of Beaurains	01/05/1916	31/05/1916
Miscellaneous	On His Majesty's Service.	04/12/1916	04/12/1916
War Diary		01/05/1916	31/05/1916
War Diary	Ronville	04/06/1916	28/06/1916
War Diary	Roclincourt	29/06/1916	30/06/1916
War Diary	Agny Near Havre	01/06/1916	30/06/1916
Heading	War Diary Of 14th Divisional Trench Mortar Batteries From 1st July 1916. To 31st July 1916 (Volume 5)		
War Diary	Roclincourt	01/07/1916	31/07/1916
War Diary	H' Sector Opposite Beaurains	01/07/1916	23/07/1916
War Diary	H. I. Section	24/07/1916	25/07/1916
War Diary	I Section	26/07/1916	31/07/1916
War Diary	J Trenches N. Of Div Scarpe	01/07/1916	30/07/1916
War Diary	A. 30 Sheet 51b NW 1	08/07/1916	31/07/1916
War Diary	Warlus	18/07/1916	18/07/1916
War Diary	Ligny-St-Flochel	19/07/1916	28/07/1916
War Diary	Arras	29/07/1916	31/07/1916
Heading	War Diary Of Medium Trench Mortar Batteries, 14th Division. From August 1st. To August 31st. (Volume VI)		
War Diary	Roclincourt	01/08/1916	03/08/1916
War Diary	Arras	03/08/1916	03/08/1916
War Diary	Lucheux	05/08/1916	05/08/1916

War Diary	Bernaville	07/08/1916	07/08/1916
War Diary	Villers Bocage	08/08/1916	08/08/1916
War Diary	Dernancourt	11/08/1916	11/08/1916
War Diary	E. 10. D. 3.5	12/08/1916	30/08/1916
War Diary		02/08/1916	30/08/1916
Heading	War Diary For August 1916 43rd Trench Mortar Battery		
War Diary	Field	01/08/1916	18/08/1916
War Diary	Field	01/08/1916	27/08/1916
War Diary	Field	18/08/1916	30/08/1916
Heading	War Diary Of Heavy Trench Mortar Battery, 14th Division. From August 1st. To August 31st (Volume 11)		
War Diary	Arras	01/08/1916	08/08/1916
War Diary	E.13.C.Central	09/08/1916	12/08/1916
War Diary	E.10.C. Central	13/08/1916	19/08/1916
War Diary	Sheet 62D E.10.C.Central	20/08/1916	30/08/1916
War Diary	E.11.C.5.7	31/08/1916	31/08/1916
Heading	War Diary Of Trench Mortar Batteries For September 1916 (Volume 111)		
War Diary	Sheet 62nd E.11 C.5.7	01/09/1916	30/09/1916
War Diary	E.11 Central	01/09/1916	30/09/1916
War Diary	Near Albert E.11.C Central	01/09/1916	05/09/1916
War Diary	S10b27	05/09/1916	12/09/1916
War Diary	F 7 C. Central	17/09/1916	18/09/1916
War Diary	S 10 C 33	19/09/1916	20/09/1916
War Diary	F7C Central	20/09/1916	24/09/1916
Heading	War Diaries Of 14th Divisional Trench Mortar Batteries From Oct 1st To October 31st 1916 Vol 7		
War Diary	E.11C. Central	02/10/1916	02/10/1916
War Diary	Bonnay	03/10/1916	03/10/1916
War Diary	Molliens	04/10/1916	04/10/1916
War Diary	Authieule	05/10/1916	05/10/1916
War Diary	Lattre St Quentin	05/10/1916	05/10/1916
War Diary	Quentin	06/10/1916	06/10/1916
War Diary	R.21 D. 10.1	08/10/1916	30/10/1916
War Diary	Meaulte	01/10/1916	01/10/1916
War Diary	Bonnay	02/10/1916	02/10/1916
War Diary	Molliens Authieulle Lattre St. Quentin	03/10/1916	06/10/1916
War Diary	Agny	07/10/1916	31/10/1916
War Diary	Meaulte Nr Albert	02/10/1916	06/10/1916
War Diary	Arras	06/10/1916	31/10/1916
War Diary	Sheet 62d E.11.c.5.7	01/10/1916	05/10/1916
War Diary	L.35.c.2.7	06/10/1916	31/10/1916
Heading	War Diary Of 14th Divisional Trench Mortar Batteries. (Medium & Heavy) From 1st November 1916. To 30th November 1916		
War Diary	Wailly	01/11/1916	30/11/1916
War Diary	Field	01/11/1916	30/11/1916
War Diary	Arras	01/11/1916	30/11/1916
War Diary	L.35.c.2.7	01/11/1916	27/11/1916
Heading	War Diary Of Trench Mortar Batteries 14th Divn. From 1st December 1916 To 31st December 1916 Vol 9		
War Diary	Wailly	02/12/1916	07/12/1916
War Diary	Ivergny	08/12/1916	31/12/1916
War Diary	C Sector Map 51B SWI Neuville Vitasse	01/12/1916	31/12/1916

War Diary	Arras lines Inf 51. B. SW I (Neuville-Vitasse) "H" Sector	01/12/1916	31/12/1916
War Diary	Dainville L.35.c.2.7	01/12/1916	06/12/1916
War Diary	Ivergny	07/12/1916	31/12/1916
Heading	War Diary Of X, Y,Z, Medium Trench Mortar Batteries From-January 1st, 1917 To-January 31st 1917 Volume 10		
War Diary	Ivergny	01/01/1917	08/01/1917
War Diary	Wailly	08/01/1917	31/01/1917
War Diary		07/01/1917	31/01/1917
War Diary	Arras	08/01/1917	31/01/1917
Heading	War Diary Of V/14 Heavy Trench Mortar Battery. From-January 1st, 1917 To-January 31st, 1917 Volume		
War Diary	Ivergny	01/01/1917	07/01/1917
War Diary	Dainville	08/01/1917	30/01/1917
Heading	War Diary Of X, Y, Z/14 Medium Trench Mortar Batteries. From 1st February, 1917 To 28th February, 1917 Volume XI		
War Diary	Wailly	01/02/1917	27/02/1917
War Diary	Arras	01/02/1917	28/02/1917
Heading	War Diary Of V/14 Heavy Trench Mortar Battery. From 1st February, 1917 to 28th February, 1917 Volume		
War Diary	Dainville L.35.c.2.7	01/02/1917	07/02/1917
War Diary	Arras G.27.b.6.0	09/02/1917	28/02/1917
Heading	War Diary Of 14th Divisional Trench Mortar Batteries, From 1st March, 1917 to-March 31st, 1917 Vol 12		
War Diary	Wailly	02/03/1917	03/03/1917
War Diary	Arras	04/03/1917	31/03/1917
War Diary	Arras	01/03/1917	31/03/1917
War Diary	Field	01/03/1917	31/03/1917
Heading	War Diary For Trench Mortar X.V.Y.& Z. Batteries 1st April To 30th 1917 Volume 24		
War Diary	Arras	01/04/1917	05/04/1917
War Diary	Simencourt	06/04/1917	16/04/1917
War Diary	Arras	17/04/1917	20/04/1917
War Diary	Wancourt	18/04/1917	21/04/1917
War Diary	Arras	25/04/1917	30/04/1917
War Diary	Arras	01/04/1917	05/04/1917
War Diary	Simencourt	06/04/1917	16/04/1917
War Diary	Arras	17/04/1917	20/04/1917
War Diary	Wancourt	18/04/1917	21/04/1917
War Diary	Arras	25/04/1917	30/04/1917
War Diary	Arras	01/04/1917	06/04/1917
War Diary	Simencourt	06/04/1917	18/04/1917
War Diary	Arras	19/04/1917	30/04/1917
War Diary	Arras	01/04/1917	06/04/1917
War Diary	Simencourt	06/04/1917	15/04/1917
War Diary	Arras	18/04/1917	30/04/1917
Heading	War Diary Of X, Y, Z And V/14 Divisional Trench Mortar Btys. From 1st May, 1917 To 31st May, 1917 Vol 14		
War Diary	Arras	01/05/1917	06/05/1917
War Diary	Achicourt	07/05/1917	31/05/1917
War Diary		01/05/1917	31/05/1917
War Diary	Arras	01/05/1917	06/05/1917

War Diary	Achicourt	07/05/1917	31/05/1917
War Diary	Arras	01/05/1917	03/05/1917
War Diary	Sheet 51B 32.c.6.4	07/05/1917	29/05/1917
War Diary	Agny	01/06/1917	27/06/1917
War Diary	Etrse-Wanien	28/06/1917	28/06/1917
War Diary	Croix	29/06/1917	30/06/1917
War Diary	Achicourt	01/06/1917	14/06/1917
War Diary	Ligny-St Flochel	15/06/1917	30/06/1917
War Diary	Field	01/06/1917	30/06/1917
War Diary	Sheet 51B 32.c.6.4	01/06/1917	30/06/1917
Heading	War Diary Of Trench Mortar Batteries, 14th Division. From July 1st, 1917 To-July 31st, 1917 Volume 27		
War Diary		01/07/1917	31/07/1917
War Diary	Croix	01/07/1917	01/07/1917
War Diary	Herne	02/07/1917	02/07/1917
War Diary	St Martin	03/07/1917	03/07/1917
War Diary	Strazeele	04/07/1917	04/07/1917
War Diary	Bailleul	05/07/1917	06/07/1917
War Diary	Dranoutre	07/07/1917	11/07/1917
War Diary	Bailleul	12/07/1917	30/07/1917
War Diary	Croix De Poperinghe	30/07/1917	31/07/1917
War Diary		01/07/1917	10/07/1917
War Diary	St Jans Capel	11/07/1917	26/07/1917
War Diary	Sheet 28 M 32.d.9.7	30/07/1917	30/07/1917
War Diary		01/07/1917	30/07/1917
Heading	War Diary For Medium And Heavy Trench Mortar Batteries 14 Division August 1917 Vol 17		
War Diary		01/08/1917	31/08/1917
War Diary	Croix De Poperinghe	01/08/1917	11/08/1917
War Diary	Reninghelst	15/08/1917	31/08/1917
War Diary	Field	01/08/1917	31/08/1917
War Diary	Croix De Poperinghe	01/08/1917	10/08/1917
War Diary	Reninghelst	11/08/1917	31/08/1917
Heading	War Diary Trench Mortar Batteries 14th Division (X/14, Y/14, Z/14 And V/14 H.T.M.) For September 1917 Vol 18		
War Diary	Reninghelst	01/09/1917	06/09/1917
War Diary	Bailleul	07/09/1917	23/09/1917
War Diary	Reninghelst	01/09/1917	06/09/1917
War Diary	Bailleul	07/09/1917	30/09/1917
War Diary	Field	01/09/1917	30/09/1917
War Diary	Reninghelst	01/09/1917	06/09/1917
War Diary	B 22.a.2.0	06/09/1917	23/09/1917
Heading	War Diary Of X/14, Y/14, Z/14, And V/14 T.M. Batteries 14th Division October-1917 Vol 19		
War Diary		03/10/1917	31/10/1917
War Diary	Bailleul	01/10/1917	11/10/1917
War Diary	Wulverghem	12/10/1917	31/10/1917
War Diary		11/10/1917	31/10/1917
War Diary	B.22.a.2 0	01/10/1917	31/10/1917
Heading	War Diary For November-1917 Trench Mortar Batteries 14th Division (X/14, Y/14, Z/14 M.T.M. Btys. & V/14 H.T.M. Bty) Vol 20		
War Diary		01/11/1917	06/11/1917
War Diary	Wulverghem	07/11/1917	30/11/1917
War Diary	Wulverghem	01/11/1917	18/11/1917

War Diary	Watou	18/11/1917	30/11/1917
War Diary	Wulverghem	01/11/1917	18/11/1917
War Diary	Watou	23/11/1917	30/11/1917
War Diary	28.t.10.d.0.4	01/11/1917	16/11/1917
War Diary	Watou	18/11/1917	26/11/1917
War Diary	Brandhoek	27/11/1917	30/11/1917
War Diary	1/4 Mile S.E.of Vlamertinghe	01/12/1917	09/12/1917
War Diary	Vlamertinghe	10/12/1917	31/12/1917
War Diary	Bradhoek Area	01/12/1917	09/12/1917
War Diary	Vlamertinghe Area	09/12/1917	31/12/1917
War Diary	Brandhoek Area	01/12/1917	10/12/1917
War Diary	Vlamertinghe	11/12/1917	31/12/1917
War Diary	Brandhoek	01/12/1917	10/12/1917
War Diary	Vlamertinghe 28.H.3.c.2.0	10/12/1917	31/12/1917
War Diary	Vlamertinghe	01/01/1918	03/01/1918
War Diary	Renescure And St Omer	04/01/1918	06/01/1918
War Diary	Etineham	07/01/1918	19/01/1918
War Diary	Corbie	20/01/1918	20/01/1918
War Diary	Valereaux	21/01/1918	31/01/1918
War Diary	Vlamertinghe	01/01/1918	02/01/1918
War Diary	Steenvoorde	03/01/1918	03/01/1918
War Diary	Renescure	04/01/1918	06/01/1918
War Diary	Etinehem	07/01/1918	24/01/1918
War Diary	Sept. Fours	25/01/1918	25/01/1918
War Diary	Guiscard	26/01/1918	30/01/1918
War Diary	Vlamertinghe	01/01/1918	06/01/1918
War Diary	Vaux En Amienois	07/01/1918	24/01/1918
War Diary	Guiscard	25/01/1918	30/01/1918
War Diary	Jussy	31/01/1918	31/01/1918
War Diary	Vlamertinghe 28.H.3.c.2.0	01/01/1918	31/01/1918
War Diary	Sheet 66.C.M.25.B.04 Fussy	03/02/1918	25/02/1918
War Diary	Sheet 66 C M 15 B 04 Fussy	01/02/1918	28/02/1918
War Diary	Minden Battacks Deepcut	17/06/1918	17/06/1918
War Diary	Minden Barracks Deepcut	04/07/1918	04/07/1918
War Diary	Folkestone	05/07/1918	05/07/1918
War Diary	Boulogne	05/07/1918	05/07/1918
War Diary	Ostrohove Rest Camp	06/07/1918	06/07/1918
War Diary	2nd Army French Mortar School	17/07/1918	20/07/1918
War Diary	Helvingham	23/07/1918	30/07/1918
Miscellaneous	To G Office 14th Divisional Headquarters	12/09/1918	12/09/1918
War Diary	Helvingham	02/08/1918	02/08/1918
War Diary	St-Sylvester Capelle	12/08/1918	12/08/1918
War Diary	Sergues (Rest Camp)	13/08/1918	13/08/1918
War Diary	Helvingham	14/08/1918	19/08/1918
War Diary	Autingues	23/08/1918	23/08/1918
War Diary	Proven (Powndon Camp)	26/08/1918	28/08/1918
War Diary	Border Camp	29/08/1918	31/08/1918
War Diary	Helvingham	02/08/1918	02/08/1918
War Diary	St-Sylvestre Capelle	12/08/1918	12/08/1918
War Diary	Serques (Rest Camp)	13/08/1918	13/08/1918
War Diary	Helvingham	14/08/1918	19/08/1918
War Diary	Autingues	23/08/1918	23/08/1918
War Diary	Proven (Powndon Camp)	26/08/1918	28/08/1918
War Diary	Border Camp	29/08/1918	31/08/1918
War Diary	Border Camp 28/A.30 Central	31/08/1918	31/08/1918
War Diary	Ypres Sector	31/08/1918	31/08/1918

War Diary	Border Camp 28/A.30 Central	01/09/1918	02/09/1918
War Diary	Ypres Sector	06/09/1918	07/09/1918
War Diary	Border Camp	07/09/1918	09/09/1918
War Diary	Cavalry Barracks Ypres Sector	12/09/1918	19/09/1918
War Diary	Border Camp	20/09/1918	20/09/1918
War Diary	Ottaiva Camp	21/09/1918	21/09/1918
War Diary	28/G24.C.6.5	22/09/1918	22/09/1918
War Diary	I.31.d.3.9 Ottawa Camp	25/09/1918	29/09/1918
War Diary	Ottawa Camp	02/10/1918	02/10/1918
War Diary	Eastwood Camp	04/10/1918	20/10/1918
War Diary	Korentje	21/10/1918	21/10/1918
War Diary	Tourcoing	28/10/1918	29/10/1918
War Diary	Train Farms	30/10/1918	30/10/1918
War Diary	Ottawa Camp 28/G.24.c.6.5	30/09/1918	19/10/1918
War Diary	Korentje 28/p.28.c.9.7 Tourcoing 28/x.29.a.b.7	21/10/1918	29/10/1918
War Diary	Trois Farm 37/u 20.d. Cent	30/10/1918	31/10/1918
War Diary	Trois Farm Coyghem 29/U 20a	01/11/1918	14/11/1918
War Diary	Wattrelos 37/a 17 C 31	14/11/1918	30/11/1918
War Diary	Wattrelos	01/12/1918	31/12/1918
War Diary	Wattrelos 37/A.17.C.3.1. 37/A.22.a.7.8	30/11/1918	19/12/1918
War Diary	Wattrelos 37/A.22.a.7.8	22/12/1918	31/12/1918
War Diary	Wattrelos	01/01/1919	22/01/1919
War Diary	Wattrelos	06/01/1919	29/01/1919

1888/1

14th Division Trench Mortar Batteries

14TH DIVISION

TRENCH MORTAR BATTERIES

JUN 1915 - JAN 1919

14 Div ~~G.H.Q. Troops~~

181/58½

29th Trench Howr Batty.

Vol I 24 — 30.6.15

Jan '19

Army Form C. 2118.

WAR DIARY
or
INTELLIGENCE SUMMARY.
(*Erase heading not required.*)

Instructions regarding War Diaries and Intelligence Summaries are contained in F. S. Regs., Part II. and the Staff Manual respectively. Title pages will be prepared in manuscript.

Place	Date	Hour	Summary of Events and Information	Remarks and references to Appendices
I 11 A. Ref. 1/40000	24.6.15	6 pm	Took over 29th T. H. Batty. of 4 1.5" Vicars T. H. Gun. Gnr. Strickland slightly wounded by H.E.	
	25.6.15	"	Reconnoitred gun positions. Placed bed of no. 2 gun to command redoubt opposite Railway Wood.	
	26.6.15	"	Fired 20 rounds at redoubt opposite Railway Wood doing considerable damage to personnel & material. Found light bombs ineffectual at ranges under 200 yds. – as giving air bursts. Also found bed of gun will sink if not placed on baulks of timber, or other large surface to distribute weight.	
	27.6.15	"	Fired 12 rounds at Redoubt opposite Y WOOD. Had two blinds, one air burst. 7 direct hits. Our support trenches heavily bombarded last night.	
	28.6.15	"	Ceased fire. Came to report personally C.R.A.	
	29.6.15	"	Returned to trench, but received Corps order to cease fire till further orders.	
	30.6.15	"	Brought guns out of action leaving beds in position under Corpl. & 2 gunners, in order to give gun crews rest. Gunner Martin wounded by shrapnel last night.	
	1.7.15		Nothing to report.	

C. S. Beecham Capt. R.F.A
Cmdg. 29th Trench Howitzer Batty.
attached C.R.A. 14th Div.

14 Dw

X 14 T M. Batt

Instructions regarding War Diaries and Intelligence Summaries are contained in F. S. Regs., Part II. and the Staff Manual respectively. Title Pages will be prepared in manuscript.

WAR DIARY
or
INTELLIGENCE SUMMARY
(Erase heading not required.)

Army Form C. 2118

Place	Date	Hour	Summary of Events and Information	Remarks and references to Appendices
VALHEUREUX	2.3.16.		X14 Trench Mortar Battery formed at 3rd Army School; and there equipped with four two inch Mortars.	
FOSSEUX	8.3.16	"	Battery moved from 3rd Army School after having completed week Course to FOSSEUX.	
DAINVILLE	11.3.16		Battery moved from FOSSEUX To DAINVILLE (Billets) Parades Daily, Inspection of Gas Helmets regular.	
do	19.3.16		Guns taken up to ARRAS.	
do	19.3.16		Emplacements made for Guns in the 41st Infantry Bde. Area.	
do	20.3.16		Two detachments in Action — Reliefs worked every Six days.	
			H. Brereton Davis LIEUT. R.F.A. O.C. X14 T.M. Bty 14 Div.	

1875 Wt. W593/826 1,000,000 4/15 J.B.C. & A. A.D.S.S./Forms/C. 2118.

Army Form C. 2118.

Instructions regarding War Diaries and Intelligence Summaries are contained in F. S. Regs., Part II. and the Staff Manual respectively. Title Pages will be prepared in manuscript.

WAR DIARY
or
~~INTELLIGENCE SUMMARY~~
(Erase heading not required.)

Y. 14 Trench Mortar Battery.
14 Div.

Place	Date	Hour	Summary of Events and Information	Remarks and references to Appendices
VALHEUREUX	2/3/16 to 8/3/16		Battery formed & week's course of instruction at III Army School	All guns were not registered in view of orders from Infantry Brigade who required instant retaliation only, both for bombs of German mortars.
FOSSEUX	9/3/16 to 11/3/16		Battery moved from III Army School. Ordinary parades carried out.	
DAINVILLE	11/3/16 to 18/3/16		Battery moved from FOSSEUX. Ordinary parades & gas helmet inspection carried out.	
	19.3.16		Inspection of trenches with view to emplacements & action.	
TRENCHES	20.3.16		Half battery to trenches – regular relief started. Emplacements proceeded with.	
	21.3.16 22.3.16 23.3.16		Emplacements made & ammunition put up.	
	24.3.16		One gun registered	
	25/3/16 to 30/3/16		Work done to emplacements, & alternative emplacements selected.	

E H Fletcher 2/Lt
O.C. Y14 TMB

2449 Wt. W14957/M90 750,000 1/16 J.B.C. & A. Forms/C.2118/12.

Z/14 TM Blr

Vol II

Confidential

Army Form C. 2118.

WAR DIARY
or
INTELLIGENCE SUMMARY
(Erase heading not required.)

Z/14 Trench Mortar B.y
14 Division

Instructions regarding War Diaries and Intelligence Summaries are contained in F. S. Regs., Part II. and the Staff Manual respectively. Title Pages will be prepared in manuscript.

Place	Date	Hour	Summary of Events and Information	Remarks and references to Appendices
Field	March 16 1/3/16		This Battery was formed at the IIIrd Army Trench Mortar School on 1st March and continued training on the guns to be used by them (2" T. Mortars) until leaving on the 8th March.	RA
	8/3/16		The Battery equipped with 4 2 inch Trench Mortars left the IIIrd Army Trench Mortar School on this date and proceeded by rail from Candas to Saulty and thence to Fosseux by road and after a few days then proceeded to Dainville preparatory to going into Action.	RA
	18/3/16		On this date the Battery was brought into Action in the area of the 43rd Infantry Brigade and emplacements were made for three guns. The following day was spent in putting these three guns into position and preparing for firing.	RA RA
	20/3		On the 20th five rounds were fired at the "Chat Maigre" (a mound in the German lines) for registration. The third round fell into enemy trench blowing up some material.	RA
	21st		The 21st was spent in building bomb stores near the emplacements.	
	22nd		On the 22nd thirteen (13) rounds were fired, five on "Chat Maigre" in retaliation for enemy Trench Mortar and eight on a barrier across the Ficheux Road in enemy lines. Firing had to be stopped on account of a heavy fall of rain which made observation impossible.	RA
	23rd		On twenty third two rounds were fired in retaliation for Enemy Trench Mortar on "Chat Maigre". The enemy immediately ceased firing	RA

2449 Wt. W14957/M90 750,000 1/16 J.B.C. & A. Forms/C.2118/12.

Army Form C. 2118.

Instructions regarding War Diaries and Intelligence Summaries are contained in F. S. Regs., Part II. and the Staff Manual respectively. Title Pages will be prepared in manuscript.

Confidential

WAR DIARY
or
~~INTELLIGENCE~~ SUMMARY

(Erase heading not required.)

Place	Date	Hour	Summary of Events and Information	Remarks and references to Appendices
	March			
Field	24		No rounds were fired on the 24th March.	R.H.
	25		On 25th five rounds were fired at enemy sapheads at "Tranchées Jocaste" to register. Good results were obtained.	R.H.
	26		On 25th March no rounds were fired.	R.H.
	27		On 27th three rounds were fired two at Sapheads B in Tranchées Jocaste and one at "Chat Maigre" which fell in enemy's lines	R.H.
	28th		Six rounds were fired at "Chat Maigre" on 28th at intervals during the day	R.H.
	30th		On 30th two rounds were fired one at "Chat Maigre" to silence trench mortar and one at saps in Tranchées Jocaste	R.H.
	31st		On 30th 13 rounds were fired. Five at barrier in enemy lines and remainder at "Chat Maigre" to stop enemy trench mortaring in retaliation	R.H.

R.E. Felton
Lt R.G.A.
O.C. Z/14 T.M. By.

2449 Wt. W14957/M90 750,000 1/16 J.B.C. & A. Forms/C.2118/12.

WAR OFFICE
RECEIVED
14 APR 1916

To/

Officer i/c. Home Records

The attached has been delayed owing to being improperly addressed

H B Davis
LT. RFA
O/C.

14th DIVISIONAL
TRENCH MORTAR
BATTERIES.

No. T.11.2
Date 11-4-16.

Confidential

Duplicate

Instructions regarding War Diaries and Intelligence Summaries are contained in F. S. Regs., Part II. and the Staff Manual respectively. Title Pages will be prepared in manuscript.

WAR DIARY
or
~~INTELLIGENCE SUMMARY~~
(Erase heading not required.)

Army Form C. 2118.

Z/14 Trench Mortar Bty.
14 Division

Place	Date March 16	Hour	Summary of Events and Information	Remarks and references to Appendices
Field	1/3/16		This Battery was formed at the III Army Trench Mortar School on 1st March and continued training on the guns to be used by them (2" T. Mortars) until leaving on the 8th March.	
	8/3/16		The Battery equipped with 4 2inch Trench Mortars left the III Army Trench Mortar School on this date and proceeded by rail from Candas to Saulty and thence to Fosseux by road and after a few days then proceeded to [illegible] preparatory to going into Action.	
	18/3/16		On this date the Battery was brought into Action in the area of the 43rd Infantry Brigade and emplacements were made for three guns. The following day was spent in putting these three guns into Action and preparing for firing.	
	20th		On the 20th four rounds were fired at the "Chat Maigre" (a mound in the German lines) for registration. The third round fell into enemy trench blowing up some material.	
	21st		The 21st was spent in building bomb stores near the emplacements.	
	22nd		On the 22nd thirteen (13) rounds were fired, four on "Chat Maigre" in retaliation for enemy Trench Mortars and eight on a "barrier" across the Ficheux Road in enemy lines. Firing had to be stopped on account of a heavy fall of rain which made observation impossible.	
	23rd		On the twenty third two rounds were fired in retaliation for enemy Trench Mortar on "Chat Maigre". The enemy immediately ceased firing.	

2449 Wt. W14957/M90 750,000 1/16 J.B.C. & A. Forms/C.2118/12.

Confidential

Duplicate

Instructions regarding War Diaries and Intelligence Summaries are contained in F. S. Regs., Part II. and the Staff Manual respectively. Title Pages will be prepared in manuscript.

WAR DIARY
or
INTELLIGENCE SUMMARY
(Erase heading not required.)

Army Form C. 2118.

Place	Date	Hour	Summary of Events and Information	Remarks and references to Appendices
Field	24		No rounds were fired on the 24th March.	RET
	25		On 25th four rounds were fired at enemy sapheads at "Tranchées Jocaste" to register. Good results were obtained.	RET
	26		On 25th March no rounds were fired.	RET
	27		On 27th three rounds were fired two at sapheads in Tranchées Jocaste and one at "Chat Marque" which fell in enemy's line	RET
	28th		Six rounds were fired at "Chat Marque" on 28th at intervals during the day	RET
	30th		On 30th two rounds were fired one at "Chat Marque" to silence trench mortar and one at saps in Tranchées Jocaste	RET
	31st		On 20th 13 rounds were fired. Five at barrier in enemy lines and remainder at "Chat Marque" to stop enemy trench mortaring in retaliation	RET

R.E. Fellin
Lt. R.G.A.
O.C. Z/14 T.M. Bty.

2449 Wt. W14957/M90 750,000 1/16 J.B.C. & A. Forms/C.2118/12.

Y 14 T M Btz

Vol II

(1)

Army Form C. 2118.

Instructions regarding War Diaries and Intelligence Summaries are contained in F. S. Regs., Part II. and the Staff Manual respectively. Title Pages will be prepared in manuscript.

WAR DIARY
or
~~INTELLIGENCE SUMMARY~~

(Erase heading not required.)

Y14 Trench Mortar Battery

Place	Date	Hour	Summary of Events and Information	Remarks and references to Appendices
	April 1st–~~2nd~~		Nothing to report	
	2nd		5 Rounds were fired in retaliation in morning and 11 in afternoon. Lt Fletcher relieved 2/Lt Aitken in battery	
	3rd	morning	5 Rounds were fired in retaliation to Enemy mortar from no 1 & 2 guns	
		afternoon	11 Rounds were fired from 2 & 4 guns in retaliation, no 2 at Enemy mortar, no 4 at trench. Enemy mortar almost directly silenced. Retaliation by Enemy with 5.9's, 30 in all one landing very near no 2 gun but just after detachment had withdrawn	
	4	morning	Alternative emplacement made ready to receive no 2 gun shed. Reserve ammunition got up from dump.	
		Afternoon	Enemy mortar opened fire Early - we retaliated with 3 rounds from no 4 gun and 1 from no 2 hitting house behind which enemy mortar seemed to be firing. Enemy mortar continued. We fired 6 Rounds from no 1 and 5 from no 3 with good results. Heavy Enemy retaliation with 5.9's. No damage.	
	5–6th		All Quiet. took opportunity of arranging that our 18 pdr batteries should open fire with us when retaliating on Enemy mortar (this was afterwards done the 18 pdr taking only a few minutes to open fire after us)	
	7th	~~#~~	~~2/Lt Aitken relieved Lt Fletcher~~ All Quiet 2/Lt Aitken relieved Lt Fletcher	
	8th		9 Rounds were fired at 5 am in retaliation to Enemy mortar. 6 were duds owing in any point to their having been fused. Explanations were asked from various quarters and it was afterwards decided not to fuze any bombs only at the shortest notice.	
	9th		17 Rounds fired in retaliation to Enemy mortar only one blind.	

2449 Wt. W14957/M90 750,000 1/16 J.B.C. & A. Forms/C.2118/12.

Instructions regarding War Diaries and Intelligence Summaries are contained in F. S. Regs., Part II. and the Staff Manual respectively. Title Pages will be prepared in manuscript.

(2)

WAR DIARY
or
INTELLIGENCE SUMMARY
(Erase heading not required.)

Army Form C. 2118.

Place	Date	Hour	Summary of Events and Information	Remarks and references to Appendices
	April 10		Fired 8 rounds in retaliation, from no 2 gun (which enemy had got no nearer to than previously mentioned) one hit sniper post, 2 rounds fired from no 3 gun. Enemy fired 20 5.9's no damage.	
	11th		Raining all day until 5 am when enemy mortar opened we replied with 5 rounds one blind.	
	12th		All quiet	
	13th		7 Rounds fired in retaliation no blinds. Lt Fletcher relieved 2/Lt Aitken	
	14th		All quiet	
	15th		Fired 2 rounds in retaliation at enemy mortar which was silenced	
	16th		Fired 4 rounds in retaliation	
	17th		No 18513 Gunner McGlauchlin was badly wounded whilst tampering with an enemy blind shell, he afterwards died. There was the usual court of inquiry. All men had been previously warned about this and were again warned. A man (gunner) came from the III Army School to [illegible] the [illegible], then [illegible].	
	18th		50 Bombs were sent up from D.A.C	
	19th		All quiet. 2/Lt Aitken relieved Lt Fletcher	
	20th		All quiet.	
	21st		9 rounds fired in retaliation. 1 blind in the morning & [illegible] in the afternoon when the enemy mortar again opened	
	22nd		At 10 am enemy opened with mortar, fired 7 rounds in retaliation, enemy opened fire again at 5.45 retaliated with 9	

2449 Wt. W14957/M90 750,000 1/16 J.B.C. & A. Forms/C.2118/12.

Army Form C. 2118.

WAR DIARY
or
INTELLIGENCE SUMMARY
(Erase heading not required.)

(3)

Instructions regarding War Diaries and Intelligence Summaries are contained in F. S. Regs., Part II. and the Staff Manual respectively. Title Pages will be prepared in manuscript.

Place	Date	Hour	Summary of Events and Information	Remarks and references to Appendices
	23rd April		All Quiet	
	24th		12 Rounds fired, 10 from no 2 and 2 from no 4. No 2 position still being intact it was decided not to use the alternative emplacement yet.	
	25th		All Quiet.	
	26th		Fired 4 rounds in retaliation	
	27th		All Quiet Lt Fletcher attend demonstration of Newton fuze at III Army School. Fired 10 rounds 6 from no 4 gun, 1 from no 3, and 3 from no 1. 2/Lt Aitken fired 20 rounds in conjunction with the artillery (covering fire) at Special Enemy work. The result of the shoot was very satisfactory & 2/Lt Aitken was congratulated by the Inf: Bde: [illegible] Lt Fletcher, whereas 2/Lt Aitken.	
	28th to 30th		All Quiet. Preparations were made for an artillery & trench mortar shoot to take place May 1st which will be reported in next diary.	
			During the month with exception of scheme with artillery, we fired only in retaliation to Enemy trench mortar, by order of the Inf: Bde. The enemy have two mortars (heavy) weighing I should think 120 lbs and caused the infantry considerable annoyance. Our retaliation throughout was quick & effective.	
			S H Fletcher Lieut O.C. Y14 Trench Mortar Battery.	

2449 Wt. W14957/M90 750,000 1/16 J.B.C. & A. Forms/C.2118/12.

XIV

Army Form C. 2118.

Instructions regarding War Diaries and Intelligence Summaries are contained in F. S. Regs., Part II. and the Staff Manual respectively. Title Pages will be prepared in manuscript.

WAR DIARY
or
~~INTELLIGENCE~~ SUMMARY
(Erase heading not required.)

X 14 T M Bty
Vol 2

Place	Date	Hour	Summary of Events and Information	Remarks and references to Appendices
BLANEY	1.5.16	5 P.M.	Relief took place.	
do	4.5.16	10 A.M.	95th I.B. relieved 41st I.B. X/14 Bty remained in Support of the former Bde.	
do	7.5.16	5 pm	Relief took place.	
do	8.5.16	—	1 Officer + 5 men on Telephonists Course.	
do	do		1 N.C.O on Gas Course.	
St Sauveur	10.5/16	9.30 pm	Fired onto Enemy's Sap - most Successful..	
Blangy + St Sauveur	11/5/16		Digging Reserve positions in ARRAS + St. Sauveur Defenses.	
Blangy	15/5/16	7 pm	Opened fire at request of Infantry.	
"	20/5/16		Retaliated for Rum Jars, Vane Bombs + Rifle Grenades.	
St Sauveur	21/5/16		Organised Shoot onto Enemy's Saps - good results. No retaliation.	
Blangy	24/5/16	10 A.M.	Retaliated for Vane Bombs. Enemy retaliated for our Mortar with 5.9 doing no damage.	
do	25/5/16	8 A.M.	No 4 gun registered onto Supposed Enemy's Dug Out from which Smoke was seen rising, Enemy retaliated whith Whizz Bangs + Rum Jars which caused us to evacuate of O.P.	
"	28/5/16	8 A.M.	No 3 gun fired onto Enemy Sap Head doing Considerable damage; Enemy retaliated with 5.9.	
St Sauveur	28/5/16	2 P.M.	Fired onto Enemy's Sap - No retaliation; 15 Rounds fired from Nos 1+2 guns in 6 minutes	
Blangy	28/5/16	3 pm	Received Orders from 95 I.B. to withdraw guns from their Area.	
Ronville	29/5/16		Digging New gun Emplacements on 42 I.B. front.	

H.B. Davis
o/c X 14 T.M. Bty

2449 Wt. W14957/M90 750,000 1/16 J.B.C. & A. Forms/C.2118/12.

XIV

Army Form C. 2118.

Instructions regarding War Diaries and Intelligence Summaries are contained in F. S. Regs., Part II. and the Staff Manual respectively. Title Pages will be prepared in manuscript.

WAR DIARY
or
~~INTELLIGENCE SUMMARY~~
(Erase heading not required.)

1.

Y/14 Trench Mortar Battery

Vol 3

Place	Date	Hour	Summary of Events and Information	Remarks and references to Appendices
Field in front of BEAURAINS	May 1st	afternoon	12 rounds were fired in conjunction with artillery (8" hows 5" 4.5 & 18 pdrs) to draw enemy mortar. Y/14 fired 12 rounds to draw mortar at 2.45 & artillery opened at 3 o'clock	
		"	The enemy mortar started shortly afterwards and after firing a few rounds ceased fire	
	2nd		2Lt Aitken relieved Lt Fletcher. 6 rounds were fired in retaliation for enemy mortar on enemy front line trenches	
	3rd		13 rounds fired in retaliation on loop holes & suspicious mound; with good effect.	
	4		11 rounds fired at mound & also enemy mortar.	
	5		16 rounds fired at X Roads in BEAURAINS in retaliation	
	6		21 rounds fired in retaliation opposite A 37 and from forward position at enemy mortar	
	7.		NIL Sgt DUFF took over from 2Lt Aitken after arrangement with unit: BOC. Lt Fletcher having taken over duties of D.O.T.M. the O.S. being on leave.	
	8		5 rounds fired in retaliation	
	9–11		No rounds fired	
	12th		Rounds fired 4 in retaliation	
	13–14		NIL	
	15		NIL 2Lt Aitken & ½ battery having completed a telephone course at WARLUS with 14 Div Signals relieved Sgt Duff.	

2449 Wt. W14957/M90 750,000 1/16 J.B.C. & A. Forms/C.2118/12.

[illegible signature] O.C. Y/14 TMB

Army Form C. 2118.

Instructions regarding War Diaries and Intelligence Summaries are contained in F. S. Regs., Part II. and the Staff Manual respectively. Title Pages will be prepared in manuscript.

WAR DIARY
or
~~INTELLIGENCE SUMMARY~~
(Erase heading not required.)

Place	Date	Hour	Summary of Events and Information	Remarks and references to Appendices
In front of BEAURAINS	16		Rounds fired 8 in retaliation, 5 from a new dug out position which proved satisfactory.	
			Cpl. KNIGHT and Pte BARTLETT were killed by a 5.9 shell whilst moving from one position to another.	
	17		5 rounds fired in retaliation	
	18		Lt Fletcher relieved 2/Lt Aiken	
	19		4 rounds were fired in conjunction with artillery at MAISON ISOLÉE which had been troubling the infantry with snipers. Good results.	
	20		New position made in dug out for retaliating on enemy mortar.	
	21		2 Rounds fired in retaliation at barrier on RONVILLE ROAD.	
	22-24		Quiet.	
	25		2/Lt Aiken relieved Lt Fletcher. 5 rounds fired.	
	26		14 rounds fired on enemy front line.	
	27-29		Lt Fletcher or Lt Aiken worked on 4 new positions on extreme left, for special shoot leaving NCO's to retaliate on right, who fired the 30 rounds.	
	30		Lt Fletcher relieved 2/Lt Aiken	
	31		Quiet.	

S H Fletcher Lieut
O.C. [illegible]

2449 Wt. W14957/M90 750,000 1/16 J.B.C. & A. Forms/C.2118/12.

ON HIS MAJESTY'S SERVICE.

FIELD POST OFFICE
A
AP 12
16
4

CENSOR

To:/

Officer i/c. Home Records.

C/O. War Office,

London.

(F. S. Reg's Part II
Confidential.)

Instructions regarding War Diaries and Intelligence Summaries are contained in F. S. Regs., Part II. and the Staff Manual respectively. Title Pages will be prepared in manuscript.

XIV

WAR DIARY
or
~~INTELLIGENCE SUMMARY~~
(Erase heading not required.)

Army Form C. 2118.

Z14 TM Bty
1

Z/14. TM BATTERY.

Vol 2

Place	Date	Hour	Summary of Events and Information	Remarks and references to Appendices
	1st May	1916	13 rounds were fired. Registration of alternate positions.	
	2nd		6 —— Ditto	
	3rd		13 — fired for registration & retaliation for enemys' mortars.	
	4th		24 rounds fired in shoot on enemy's saps & front line.	
	5th		Nil. Digging new emplacement on left of sector.	
	6th		Offensive 24 rounds fired from 2 guns. Enemy retaliated with heavies & killed Gnr R H Wilson & buried the mortar.	
	7 & 8.		No firing. Buried Gnr WILSON, on 7th May.	
	9.		5 Rounds fired in retaliation for mortars	
	10.		8 Rounds in retaliation "	
	11		14 Rounds fired in retaliation. "	
	12 & 13.			
	14. 15 16		Retaliation for mortars. 32 rounds fired.	
	17.		Combined shoot with artillery on enemys front line. Fired 23 rounds.	
	18		enemy retaliated with 5"9s & buried one mortar.	
	19 20		Nil. Digging fresh emplacements.	
	21st		2 rounds retaliation	
	22 23 24 25		Digging reserve emplacements well back to cover supposed enemys mine.	
	26.		Enemy brought up two heavy minenwerfer & fired into our support line. we retaliated with 3 rounds silencing him.	

2449 Wt. W14957/M90 750,000 1/16 J.B.C. & A. Forms/C.2118/12.

Army Form C. 2118.

Instructions regarding War Diaries and Intelligence Summaries are contained in F. S. Regs., Part II. and the Staff Manual respectively. Title Pages will be prepared in manuscript.

WAR DIARY
or
~~INTELLIGENCE SUMMARY~~

(Erase heading not required.)

Z/14. T.M.B.

Place	Date	Hour	Summary of Events and Information	Remarks and references to Appendices
	27 } 28 }		Registered reserve emplacement	
	29		Digging.	
	30. 31.		Retaliated for enemy heavy mortar	

E G Porter 2nd Lieut.
for OC Z/14 TM Battery.

2449 Wt. W14957/M90 750,000 1/16 J.B.C. & A. Forms/C.2118/12.

Instructions regarding War Diaries and Intelligence Summaries are contained in F. S. Regs., Part II. and the Staff Manual respectively. Title Pages will be prepared in manuscript.

WAR DIARY
or
~~INTELLIGENCE SUMMARY~~
(Erase heading not required.)

Army Form C. 2118.

June 1st to 30th 1916.
X/14 T.M.By.

Vol 3

Place	Date	Hour	Summary of Events and Information	Remarks and references to Appendices
RONVILLE	4th	4 p.m.	Registered Enemy's Sap at M5. a. 6. 7½. Enemy retaliated the following morning with 65/5.9 Shells on to Mortar Emplacement – doing no damage at all.	
"	5	8.30 p.m.	Registering M5. a. 3. 8. Enemy's Entrance to Sap. Enemy retaliated immediately with whizz bangs.	
"	7	5 p.m.	Relief took place.	
"	9	3.15 p.m.	Special shoot arranged by 42nd I.B. Enemy retaliated with Whizz Bangs & Small T. Ms. We continued firing till hostile T. Ms. ceased firing.	
"	10	3 p.m.	Fired in retaliation for Enemy's heavy Mortar at BEAURAINS, Enemy Counter retaliated with Small T. Ms & 77 M.M. shells. We continued firing until Enemy ceased firing	
"	11	2 p.m.	Fired in retaliation onto Y. Sap. M5. a. 6. 7½.	
"	13	5 p.m.	Relief took place. Fired in retaliation for Enemy's Heavy Minenwerfer at BEAURAINS at 7 p.m. until Enemy ceased fire.	
"	13.		2nd/Lt. C. C. O. TAYLOR transferred to Command V/14 By, was Superseded by 2nd/Lt. A. W. BENTLEY R.F.A.	
"	14		Six new Alternative positions & O.Ps. being prepared.	
"	16	4 p.m.	Retaliated heavily for Enemy's T. Ms & Minenwerfers.	

2449 Wt. W14957/M90 750,000 1/16 J.B.C. & A. Forms/C.2118/12.

Instructions regarding War Diaries and Intelligence Summaries are contained in F. S. Regs., Part II. and the Staff Manual respectively. Title Pages will be prepared in manuscript.

WAR DIARY
or
~~INTELLIGENCE SUMMARY~~
(Erase heading not required.)

June 1st to 30th 1916
X/14 T.M. Bty.

Army Form C. 2118.

Place	Date	Hour	Summary of Events and Information	Remarks and references to Appendices
RONVILLE	~~22~~ (21)	5pm	Registered Barrier on RONVILLE ROAD with NEWTON delay action Fuze, most Satisfactory results. M4. D8.9.	
"	24	—	Fired in retaliation for Enemy's Minenwerfers; Enemy Counter retaliated with Small T.Ms. these were soon Silenced with our Newton percussion fuzes.	
"	26	3pm	Fired in conjunction with 14 D.H. Operation Orders Nos 19–23. Fired on to Enemy's wire with Newton percussion fuzes much wire was cut.	
"	27	5 A.M.	Fired at intervals from 5 A.M. to 12.30pm onto Enemy's wire a great quantity of the Enemy's wire was cut at:– M5-a. 0.1½ and M5-a 7½–8¼. also at M5-B. 1.8¾ + 9.35 & 5¾.1. Enemy retaliated heavily with 77 MM. 105 M.M. + 150 MM Shells – doing little damage.	
"	28	8.30pm	Received Orders to withdraw from 42 I.B. and to go into Support of 41st I.B.	
ROCLINCOURT	29	—	Preparing positions in new Area.	
"	30	—	" " " " "	

H.B. Davis
Lt. R.F.A.
O/C X/14 T.M. Bty
14 Div.

2449 Wt. W14957/M90 750,000 1/16 J.B.C. & A. Forms/C.2118/12.

Original

Instructions regarding War Diaries and Intelligence Summaries are contained in F. S. Regs., Part II. and the Staff Manual respectively. Title Pages will be prepared in manuscript.

WAR DIARY
or
~~INTELLIGENCE SUMMARY~~
(Erase heading not required.)

Z/14 T. M. Bty.

Vol 3

Army Form C. 2118.

Place	Date	Hour	Summary of Events and Information	Remarks and references to Appendices
Agny near Arras	June 1916 1		No rounds were fired.	
	2		3 rounds fired in retaliation for enemy mortars.	
	3		7 do do	
	4		7 do do	
	5		No rounds fired.	
	6		No rounds fired	
	7		27 rounds fired in retaliation for enemy Minenwerfers	
	8		3 rounds fired in retaliation for mortars	
	9			
	10		6 do do	
			5 do do	
	11		14 do fired in retaliation for Minenwerfer	
	12		No rounds fired	
	13		7 rounds fired in retaliation	
	14		15 do do for Minenwerfer.	
	15 } 16 } 17 }		No rounds were fired on these dates. Gun new positions were selected and completed in order to take part in a scheme by 14 D.A.	
	18		3 rounds fired	
	19		25 rounds fired in retaliation for enemy Minenwerfer	
	20		21 do do do	

2449 Wt. W14957/M90 750,000 1/16 J.B.C. & A. Forms/C.2118/12.

Army Form C. 2118.

WAR DIARY
or
~~INTELLIGENCE SUMMARY~~
(Erase heading not required.)

Instructions regarding War Diaries and Intelligence Summaries are contained in F. S. Regs., Part II. and the Staff Manual respectively. Title Pages will be prepared in manuscript.

Z/14 T M Bty

Place	Date	Hour	Summary of Events and Information	Remarks and references to Appendices
	June 16 21		No rounds were fired.	
	22		11 rounds were fired from two guns in retaliation for enemy Minenwerfer. The sixth round from one of these guns burst in the muzzle but no casualties were sustained. Owing to the tail sticking in the bore the gun was put out of Action.	
	23		On this day 200 rounds were fired in conjunction with 14 D. H. Operation orders No 19. Target; Enemy wire between M 14 C 9 and M 20 a. 1·3½. Sheet 51 B ~~Noyon~~ Firing from three guns, commenced at 4.30 A.M. and continued at intervals throughout the day until 8 p.m. Fire was distributed across the whole area, special attention being paid to the Enemy Saps which at the end of the day looked decidedly dilapidated. Some gaps were made in front wire.	
	24		In continuance of 14 D.H. Operation Order No 19. 200 rounds were again fired on this day. It was noticed that some of the gaps of yesterday were no longer visible as they had been rewired during the night.	

2449 Wt. W14957/M90 750,000 1/16 J.B.C. & A. Forms/C.2118/12.

Instructions regarding War Diaries and Intelligence Summaries are contained in F. S. Regs., Part II. and the Staff Manual respectively. Title Pages will be prepared in manuscript.

WAR DIARY

or

~~INTELLIGENCE SUMMARY~~

(Erase heading not required.)

2/14 T. M. Bty

Army Form C. 2118.

Place	Date	Hour	Summary of Events and Information	Remarks and references to Appendices
	June 1916 24th		Firing was carried out at intervals throughout the day starting at 5.30 am and ending at 8 p.m. Enemy was very active with his Heavy and Medium Minenwerfers during the day, and it would seem that he expended his supply of ammunition as he stopped firing before we did on two occasions. Wire was cut in the main front line this day, and although observation was exceedingly difficult owing to the length of the grass, a large area was visible at which no wire was left on the stakes and in some places stakes are missing.	
	25th		300 rounds were again fired on this day in continuation of the Scheme of the preceding days. Firing started at 5.30 and finished at 8 pm. Direct hits were made on Saps H. B. C and D in Enemy line and more wire was cut.	
	26th		309 rounds were fired in conclusion of scheme on this day	

2449 Wt. W14957/M90 750,000 1/16 J.B.C. & A. Forms/C.2118/12.

Army Form C. 2118.

Instructions regarding War Diaries and Intelligence Summaries are contained in F. S. Regs., Part II. and the Staff Manual respectively. Title Pages will be prepared in manuscript.

WAR DIARY
or
~~INTELLIGENCE SUMMARY~~
(Erase heading not required.)

Z/14 T.M. Bty

Place	Date	Hour	Summary of Events and Information	Remarks and references to Appendices
	June 1916 26		Firing started at 6.30 and finished at 9.30. At the conclusion no wire was visible on Saps B and D. and large gaps were apparent in the front wire. Delay action fuzes were used against the barrier on the Ficheux Rd and a large quantity of timber and material was displaced by explosions.	
			When firing was completed the guns were removed from their emplacements and the battery returned to DAINVILLE	
	27th		on the morning of the 27th	
			On the evening of the 27th the Battery again went into action with the 43rd Inf. Bde who were in the line at I and J sectors.	
	28th		Two guns were put into positions left by X/15 T.M. By and on	
	29		the following day the remaining two guns were put into position and 8 rounds were fired for registration. The firing of these rounds was the signal for several German Trench Mortars and Minenwerfer	

2449 Wt. W14957/M90 750,000 1/16 J.B.C. & A. Forms/C.2118/12.

Army Form C. 2118.

Instructions regarding War Diaries and Intelligence Summaries are contained in F. S. Regs., Part II. and the Staff Manual respectively. Title Pages will be prepared in manuscript.

WAR DIARY
or
~~INTELLIGENCE SUMMARY~~

(Erase heading not required.)

Z/14 T.M. Bty

Place	Date	Hour	Summary of Events and Information	Remarks and references to Appendices
	29		[gun to open fire] And a direct hit was made on the emplacement.	R.E.F.
	30		No rounds were fired and a new position was selected to replace that [for the gun] which had been knocked out the day before.	
			R. E. Felton 2/Lt R.G.A. O.C. Z/14 T.M.By.	

2449 Wt. W14957/M90 750,000 1/16 J.B.C. & A. Forms/C.2118/12.

CONFIDENTIAL

WAR DIARY

OF

14TH DIVISIONAL TRENCH MORTAR BATTERIES

From 1st July 1916. To 31st July 1916.

=*=*=*=*=*==*=

(Volume 5)

Instructions regarding War Diaries and Intelligence Summaries are contained in F. S. Regs., Part II. and the Staff Manual respectively. Title Pages will be prepared in manuscript.

WAR DIARY

or

~~INTELLIGENCE SUMMARY~~

(Erase heading not required.)

Original

July 1st – 31st 1916

X/14 Trench Mortar Battery

Vol 4

Army Form C. 2118.

Place	Date	Hour	Summary of Events and Information	Remarks and references to Appendices
ROCLINCOURT	1st	–	Digging new emplacements at G.6.C.2.7. G6.A.2.8 and A30. C.3.2.	MAP REF:- 51B. N.W.1 + 51B. N.W.3.
"	2	–	working on new positions.	
"	3	–	Registered No 1 Gun at G.6.C.2.7.	
"	4	–	do No 2 " " G.6.A.2.8. Fired in retaliation for Enemy's Small mortars.	
"	5	3-4.30pm	Heavy shelling by 5.9 & 4.2 shells. Fired 20 rounds in retaliation for Small Mortars.	
"	7 & 8		Relief took place. Rained heavily.	
"	9		All Quiet. Carrying on with improvements to positions.	
	10		All Quiet.	
"	11		Retaliated for Minenwerfers. No 1 gun heavily shelled with 77MM & 105-MM Shells.	
"	12		Laying telephone wires.	
"	13		Relief took place.	
"	14		Put in temporary Emplacement while no 1 gun position was being repaired	
"	15		Registered temporary emplacement.	
	16		2/Lt. A.W. BENTLEY R.F.A transferred to Z/14 Bty; and superseded by 2/Lt J. G. WALSER R.F.A.	
"	17		from B/48 Bde. R.F.A	
"	18.		Relief took place.	
"	19		Fired in retaliation for Enemy's Vane Bombs.	
"	20		" " " " " Minenwerfers.	
"	21		" " " " " Light mortars.	
"	22		" " " " " " "	
			No 3 gun out of action, Rifle mechanism blown out.	
			Br. PRICE recalled to England for Munition works.	

2449 Wt. W14957/M90 750,000 1/16 J.B.C. & A. Forms/C.2118/12.

Instructions regarding War Diaries and Intelligence Summaries are contained in F. S. Regs., Part II. and the Staff Manual respectively. Title Pages will be prepared in manuscript.

WAR DIARY
or
~~INTELLIGENCE SUMMARY~~
(Erase heading not required.)

Army Form C. 2118.

Place	Date	Hour	Summary of Events and Information	Remarks and references to Appendices
ROCLINCOURT	23		Fired in retaliation for Enemy's Minenwerfers.	
"	24		Fired 40 rounds in conjunction with 41/I.B. orders. No. 3 gun out of action.	
			No. 1 gun replaced No 3 at G.6. A2.8.	
"	25		Improving No 1 gun emplacement.	
"	26		Digging alternative position for No 3 gun.	
"	27	5 to pm	Relief took place. Fired in retaliation for Minenwerfers.	
"	28		all Quiet.	
"	29		41/I.B. relieved by 84/I.B.	
			Received G.O.C. 41/I.B. congratulations to Battery for all good work done while in support of the 41/I.B.	
"	30		Fired in retaliation for Minenwerfers.	
"	31.		" " " " "	

H B Davis
Lt. R.F.A.
ofc × 114 T M By.

Y/14 Trench Mortar Batt   July 1916   Original   Army Form C. 2118.

Vol 4

WAR DIARY
or
INTELLIGENCE SUMMARY
(Erase heading not required.)

Instructions regarding War Diaries and Intelligence Summaries are contained in F. S. Regs., Part II. and the Staff Manual respectively. Title Pages will be prepared in manuscript.

Place	Date	Hour	Summary of Events and Information	Remarks and references to Appendices
"H" Sector opposite Beaumont	July 1/16	7 a.m	In conjunction with Artillery opened fire at 7 a.m during smoke screen. Fired 183 rounds from 4 guns continuing from 7 - 8 a.m at the following objectives (a) 1 gun - at "Y" sap & adjacent front line (b) 1 " - Front line from M4d 5-9½ to M4d 5.7 (c) 2 "s - " " and patrol from M4d 5.1 to M4d 6.3	
	July 2		Quiet day - no firing done - worked at repairs to positions damaged in previous weeks shooting & in replenishing ammunition. 2nd Lt Aiken relieved 2nd Lt. Jaylor	
	" 3		no firing done.	
	" 4	10-11 am	Fired 19 rounds in retaliation to German mortars, on front & support lines opposite H.32	
	" 5		Quiet day - no firing	
	" 6		" " " "	
	" 7		" " " " 2nd Lt Jaylor relieved 2nd Lt Aiken	
	" 8		Fired 46 rounds in retaliation	
	" 9		no firing - ammunition brought forward & distributed	
	" 10		" " " " " "	

Army Form C. 2118.

Instructions regarding War Diaries and Intelligence Summaries are contained in F. S. Regs., Part II. and the Staff Manual respectively. Title Pages will be prepared in manuscript.

WAR DIARY
or
INTELLIGENCE SUMMARY

(Erase heading not required.)

Place	Date	Hour	Summary of Events and Information	Remarks and references to Appendices
"H" Sector opposite Beaumains	July 11		Fired 87 rounds in conjunction with artillery in the afternoon. Kept on firing after shoot till Hun mortar was silenced. 2nd Lt Asker relieved 2nd Lt Taylor.	
	" 12		Fired 55 rounds commencing at 2 p.m. in conjunction with artillery in bombardment of Beaumains as follows:- (a) 25 rounds M 4 d 5½.6 – M 4 d 5½.9 (b) 30 " M 5 a 7.8 + vicinity. Much damage done to enemy's trenches	
	" 13		In accordance with wire cutting scheme to simulate attack on Ficheux – Beaumains front:- fired as follows from 7.10 till 9.15 p.m. (a) 40 rounds into wire at M 4 d 5.9½ (b) 12 " " " in front of Y sap. } Much damage done to wire	
	" 14	3 a.m.	Fired 74 rounds from 3 guns during bombardment with smoke screen continuing from 3 – 4 a.m. on following points (a) "Y" sap + adjacent front line (b) German trench on right of Ronville. Beaumains Rd (c) German front line opposite H 32.	

2449 Wt. W14957/M90 750,000 1/16 J.B.C. & A. Forms/C.2118/12.

Instructions regarding War Diaries and Intelligence Summaries are contained in F. S. Regs., Part II. and the Staff Manual respectively. Title Pages will be prepared in manuscript.

3

WAR DIARY
or
INTELLIGENCE SUMMARY
(Erase heading not required.)

Army Form C. 2118.

Place	Date	Hour	Summary of Events and Information	Remarks and references to Appendices
"H" Section opposite Beaumont	July 15	10.30	Fired 9 rounds in retaliation During the afternoon fired 51 rounds into wire at left of Beaumont crossroads at request of OC 5th K.S.L.I. also fired 26 rounds in retaliation at Y sap & vicinity. Lt Taylor transferred to "Z" Battery	
	" 16		In accordance with instructions received from 42nd I.B. fired 50 rounds into enemy's wire as follows (a) 30 rounds into wire in vicinity of M4d 5.9½ (b) 20 " " " in front of "Y" sap 5 rounds fired opposite H32 in retaliation	
	" 17 } 18 } 19 }		Quiet - no firing done - work begun on new emplacements	
	" 20		Fired 12 rounds in retaliation	
	" 21		No 7513 Gr Turner wounded	
	" 22		On night of 22/23 two guns taken out & moved to I section	
	" 23		Worked at new emplacements in I section - rushed up ammunition & had 2 guns in position by stand-to on morning of 24th.	

Instructions regarding War Diaries and Intelligence Summaries are contained in F. S. Regs., Part II. and the Staff Manual respectively. Title Pages will be prepared in manuscript.

WAR DIARY
or
INTELLIGENCE SUMMARY
(Erase heading not required.)

Army Form C. 2118.

Place	Date	Hour	Summary of Events and Information	Remarks and references to Appendices
'H' & 'I' Sectors	July 24		Quiet on both sectors – no firing	
	" 25		On night of 25/26 remaining 2 guns & personnel removed from 'H' sector	
I sector	" 26			
	" 27		worked on new emplacements in I sector.	
	28		Lt. Fletcher returned to duty from Hospital on evening of 28th.	
	29			
	30			
	31			

J D Archer 2nd Lt.
Y 14 Trench Mortar Battery

2449 Wt. W14957/M90 750,000 1/16 J.B.C. & A. Forms/C.2118/12.

Z/14 Trench Mortar Batt — July 1916 — Original

WAR DIARY

~~or~~

~~INTELLIGENCE SUMMARY~~

(Erase heading not required.)

Army Form C. 2118.

Vol 4

Instructions regarding War Diaries and Intelligence Summaries are contained in F. S. Regs., Part II. and the Staff Manual respectively. Title Pages will be prepared in manuscript.

Place	Date	Hour	Summary of Events and Information	Remarks and references to Appendices
Trenches N. of River SCARPE	1-7-16.	5 pm.	Fired 31 rounds in registration of four new positions	
	2-7-16.	11 am.	Fired 5 rounds to draw enemy's heavy mortars without success.	
	4-7-16.	4-30 pm	Fired 4 rounds in retaliation for enemy's heavy mortar which ceased fire.	
	7-7-16.		Fired 19 rounds in retaliation for enemy's mortars.	
	10-7-16.		Fired 31 " " " . Lieut. GODSON joined the battery from A/46 Bde RFA. 2/Lieut. E G PORTER left the battery on taking command of a ~~heavy~~ temporary battery in K2.	
	12-7-16.		Fired 21 rounds in retaliation for enemy's mortars. Lieut. GODSON admitted to hospital suffering from shell shock.	
	14-7-16.		Lieut. R.E. FELTON left the battery on appointment to 60th Div as D.O.T.M.	
	15-7-16.		2/Lieut. C.C.O. TAYLOR took the command of the battery vice Lt. FELTON. 2/Lieut. A.W. BENTLEY transferred from X/14 to Z/14 T.M. Battery. 2/Lt. TAYLOR went up to trenches.	
	16-7-16.		New site chosen to cover suspected enemy mine at Fire trench J.95.	
	17-7-16.		Relief of battery took place.	
	18-7-16.		2/Lt. Bentley relieved 2/Lt. Taylor. Fired 5 rounds in retaliation for enemy mortars.	
	19-7-16.		Fired 82 rounds with 3 guns in combined shoot with 6" Howitzers.	
	20-7-16.		Prepared position at J99 to cover G12a56.	

2449 Wt. W14957/M90 750,000 1/16 J.B.C. & A. Forms/C.2118/12.

Army Form C. 2118.

WAR DIARY
or
INTELLIGENCE SUMMARY

(Erase heading not required.)

Instructions regarding War Diaries and Intelligence Summaries are contained in F. S. Regs., Part II. and the Staff Manual respectively. Title Pages will be prepared in manuscript.

Place	Date	Hour	Summary of Events and Information	Remarks and references to Appendices
	21-7-16		J99 position completed. One 1½" gun placed in Mark Avenue to cover Six ARBRES	
	22-7-16	4-30pm	Fired 63 two inch rounds + 37 1½" rounds in retaliation to enemy mortars which finally closed fire	
	23-7-16		Relief took place. ~~Enemy~~ Enemy opened fire at 9 am with four 110lb mortars & continued at intervals till 8-30 pm. Two 2" guns retaliated with 84 rounds & the 1½" gun with 52 rounds. One 2" gun was out of action during the middle part of the day due to the breaking of a rifle mechanism. A spare mechanism was obtained by 5 pm. At 9-30 pm the enemy suddenly opened an intense bombardment behind J81 to J84 the 1½" gun being buried at the commencement. Both 2" guns ~~had~~ were out of action due to broken bolts. The crews therefore stood by their guns in readiness to take them out of action – this was not found to be necessary however.	
	24-7-16		Received orders to prepare two 2" guns & one 1½" gun to fire on G18C24. This was done the guns being ready to fire at nightfall.	
	25-7-16		The 2" fired 32 rounds & the 1½" fired 22 rounds at enemy's barrier at G18C24. Sgt: Ebry & Br Gaywood were killed by 4.2 shrapnel & Gnr Leatherland wounded. Gnrs Dennerly, Martin, Christie, Warland, Worsick & Willey were wounded by a 2" bomb which	

2449 Wt. W14957/M90 750,000 1/16 J.B.C. & A. Forms/C.2118/12.

Army Form C. 2118.

Instructions regarding War Diaries and Intelligence Summaries are contained in F. S. Regs., Part II. and the Staff Manual respectively. Title Pages will be prepared in manuscript.

WAR DIARY

~~or~~

~~INTELLIGENCE SUMMARY~~

(Erase heading not required.)

Place	Date	Hour	Summary of Events and Information	Remarks and references to Appendices
			exploded on leaving the gun.	
	26-7-16.		Gnr Leatherland + Gnr Dennerly died in hospital of wounds.	
	28-7-16		62nd Inf: Bde: relieved 43rd Inf: Bde: in this sector	
	29-7-16.		Battery relief took place.	
	30-7-16.		21st D.O.T.M. visited the sector + gun positions.	

C. C. O. Taylor, Lt.

O.C. 2/14 T.M.B.

31-7-16.

2449 Wt. W14957/M90 750,000 1/16 J.B.C. & A. Forms/C.2118/12.

Original Army Form C. 2118.

July 1916

Vol I

WAR DIARY

or

INT~~ELLIGENCE SUMMARY~~

(*Erase heading not required.*)

NEW. T. M. B.

Instructions regarding War Diaries and Intelligence Summaries are contained in F. S. Regs., Part II. and the Staff Manual respectively. Title Pages will be prepared in manuscript.

Place	Date	Hour	Summary of Events and Information	Remarks and references to Appendices
A.30 — Sheet — 51B NW 1	8/7/16		4 · 2 inch guns complete with 8 beds arrived.	
	10/7/16.		The 50% trained personnel arrived from 3rd Army School of Mortars.	
	11/7/16, 12 –, 13 –, 14 –, 15 –		Time spent in digging positions & dug-outs. 2nd LT. C.M. SANDEL relieved 2nd LT. E.G. PORTER.	
	16.		Fired 13 rounds. Registration.	
	17.		Registration on enemy's front line, about which much work had been upsiled. (MAP reference) A 30 c. 6.8)	
	18.		Fired 23 rounds. Destroyed enemy's sniper post.	
	19.		Fired 37 rounds at emplacement behind front line. Direct hits being obtained.	
	20.		2nd LT S.M. SANDEL was relieved by 2nd LT E.G. PORTER. Fired 8 rounds retaliation in front of KING Crater, much timber thrown about. 1½ inch gun sent up to fire off all 1½ ammunition left over in trenches.	
	21st		Retaliated for vane bombs. 3 2 inch rounds & 11. 1½ inch fired.	
	~~22nd~~ 23rd		Fired 8 2 inch & 36 1½ inch bombs in retaliation. Very effective.	
			Fired 7 rounds in retaliation.	
	24.		Fired in retaliation 19 2 inch & 30 1½ inch. Also fired on working party in front of KING crater (A 30 c 6.6) Working stopped.	
	~~25~~ 25th		Shoot arranged with 18 pdrs & 4.5 Hows. Fired on work at (A 30 c 6.8) also work in front of KING crater. Fired 53 2 inch & 26 1½ inch.	

Army Form C. 2118.

Instructions regarding War Diaries and Intelligence Summaries are contained in F. S. Regs., Part II. and the Staff Manual respectively. Title Pages will be prepared in manuscript.

WAR DIARY
or
~~INTELLIGENCE SUMMARY~~

(Erase heading not required.)

Place	Date	Hour	Summary of Events and Information	Remarks and references to Appendices
26/7/16			2 Lt. C.M. Samuel relieved 2nd Lt E.G. PORTER	
27/7/16			12 rounds 2 inch during the night, at enemy's working party in front of KING crater & A30 c 6.8. Fired 34 1½ inch rounds in retaliation for vane bombs during the day.	
	28/7/16		Enemy brought up a medium minenwerfer & opened fire at 6.15 pm. We retaliated 16 rounds of 2 inch causing timber & revetting frames to fly up into the air. Effectively stopped hostile mortar fire.	
	29/7/16		Enemy started firing with minenwerfer about 7 pm. We retaliated heavily for mortars & 7.7 MM & 4.2". We did considerable damage to enemy's trenches having several direct hits. Infantry reported working party ~~at 10 AM~~ left of KING crater working on his trenches during the night. This was one of the points fired on, where considerable damage was done.	
	30/7/16		Rounds fired 2 in retaliation for vane bombs.	
	31/7/16		Fired 47 rounds 2 inch in retaliation for 12 ~~heavy~~ medium minenwerfers & vane bombs. we continued shooting after the enemy ceased firing. E.G. Porter 2nd Lieut. NEW T.M. Battery 2nd Lt E.G. PORTER relieved 2nd Lt C.M. SAMUEL	

2449 Wt. W14957/M90 750,000 1/16 J.B.C. & A. Forms/C.2118/12.

Volume I

Original

Army Form C. 2118

WAR DIARY
or
~~INTELLIGENCE SUMMARY~~
(Erase heading not required.)

Instructions regarding War Diaries and Intelligence Summaries are contained in F. S. Regs., Part II. and the Staff Manual respectively. Title Pages will be prepared in manuscript.

July 1916

V/14 Heavy Trench Mortar Battery

Vol I

Place	Date	Hour	Summary of Events and Information	Remarks and references to Appendices
WARLUS	18th		Battery formed. Authority 14th D.A. 2580/2 dated 17.7.16.	
			Lieut. E.G.F. Gunning (A/49) being given Command.	
			2nd Lt. A.S.H. Taylor (A/46) 2nd Lt. N.D.E. Lowe (B/46) posted to Battery.	
			Rank + File posted from Units of 14th D.A.	
			Battery proceeds to School of Mortars, 3rd Army at LIGNY-ST-FLOCHEL for Course of Training	
LIGNY-ST-FLOCH-EL	19th		Battery at School of Mortars, 3rd Army on Course of Training	
	20th		" " "	
	21		" " "	
	22		" " "	
	23		" " "	
	24		" " "	
	25		" " "	
	26		" " "	
	27		" " "	
	28th		Battery proceeds to billets in Arras having completed Course of Training.	
ARRAS	29		Battery at rest in billets in ARRAS.	
	30		" " " " " " "	
	31		" " " " " " "	

E.G.F. Gunning
Lieut. R.F.A.
Comdg. V/14 Heavy T. M. Battery.

1875 Wt. W593/826 1,000,000 4/15 J.B.C. & A. A.D.S.S./Forms/C. 2118.

Vols 5

C O N F I D E N T I A L

=*=*=*=*=*=*=*=*=*=*=*=

W A R   D I A R Y

O F

MEDIUM TRENCH MORTAR BATTERIES, 14TH DIVISION.

From August 1st.   To August 31st.

(VOLUME V1)

=*=*=*=*=

Army Form C. 2118.

Instructions regarding War Diaries and Intelligence Summaries are contained in F. S. Regs., Part II. and the Staff Manual respectively. Title Pages will be prepared in manuscript.

WAR DIARY

~~or~~

~~INTELLIGENCE SUMMARY~~

(Erase heading not required.)

X/14 T. M. Bty

August 1st - 31st 1916

Place	Date	Hour	Summary of Events and Information	Remarks and references to Appendices
ROCLINCOURT.	1st		Officers relief took place. All Quiet. Improving positions & digging Alternative position for No 2 gun.	
"	2nd		Fired 61 rounds in retaliation for Enemy's Minenwerfers – Much damage was done to the Enemy's wire by the Newton Percussion fuzes.	
"	3rd	2 P.M.	Relieved by 21st DIV. X/21 Bty; handed guns over to same.	
ARRAS	3		Midnight Battery left in Lorries for LUCHEUX – Billets.	
LUCHEUX	5.	9 A.M.	Left for BERNAVILLE. Billets.	
BERNAVILLE	7		Left for VILLERS BOCAGE. Billets.	
VILLERS BOCAGE	8.		Left for DERNANCOURT. Bivouacs.	
DERNANCOURT.	11		Pitched camp alongside River Ancre. Bivouacs. E10. d 3 5.	
E.10. d 3. 5.	12 - 19		Usual parades carried out.	
	20		X/14 Bty Relieved 17 Div. Z/17 Bty at Carlton Terrace.	
	23		Digging Gun positions under heavy Shell fire at DORSET + BLACKWATCH trenches. Gnr. BUTLER wounded Shell Shock.	
			Gnr DRISCOLL Shrapnel wounds.	
	24		Fired onto Wood Lane + Tea trench in conjunction with Special Operation Orders of the 33rd DIVISION.	
	25		Relieved by Z/14 Bty.	

2449 Wt. W14957/M90 750,000 1/16 J.B.C. & A. Forms/C.2118/12.

Instructions regarding War Diaries and Intelligence Summaries are contained in F. S. Regs., Part II. and the Staff Manual respectively. Title Pages will be prepared in manuscript.

WAR DIARY
or
~~INTELLIGENCE SUMMARY~~

(Erase heading not required.)

Army Form C. 2118.

X/14 T. M. By.
August 1st – 31st 1916

Place	Date	Hour	Summary of Events and Information	Remarks and references to Appendices
	30th.		Half the Battery left for Trenches to relieve Z/14 By. Rained Heavily.	

H B Davis
OC X/14 T.M.By.

2449 Wt. W14957/M90 750,000 1/16 J.B.C. & A. Forms/C.2118/12.

Army Form C. 2118.

WAR DIARY
or
INTELLIGENCE SUMMARY
(Erase heading not required.)

Instructions regarding War Diaries and Intelligence Summaries are contained in F. S. Regs., Part II. and the Staff Manual respectively. Title Pages will be prepared in manuscript.

Place	Date	Hour	Summary of Events and Information	Remarks and references to Appendices
	2-8-16.		2/Lieut. TAYLOR relieved 2/Lt: BENTLEY who returned to Battery.	
	3-8-16.		21st Div. trench Mortar officers took over the line relieving 2/14 T.M.B. at midday.	
			Left ARRAS at midnight for LUCHEUX.	
	5-8-16		Left LUCHEUX for BERNAVILLE which was reached at Noon.	
	7-8-16		Left BERNAVILLE for VILLERS – BOCAGE.	
	8-8-16.		Left VILLERS-BOCAGE for BUIRE where the Battery was encamped until 11-8-16.	
	11-8-16.		Moved camp to a site about 1 mile S. of ALBERT where the battery made permanent bivouacks.	
	25-8-16		2/Lt: PORTER + half battery relieved Lieut. TAYLOR at CARLTON TRENCH West of DELVILLE WOOD, in support of 33rd Div:	
	28-8-16.		Lieut: TAYLOR + half battery took 3 guns to BERNAFAY WOOD in readiness to cover ALE ALLEY East of DELVILLE WOOD. The guns were not needed at the time + were left at BERNAFAY WOOD under a guard the remainder of the detachment returning to camp.	
	30-8-16		2/Lt: PORTER + half battery relieved by 2/Lt: WALSER.	

C. C. O. Taylor Lieut:
O.C. 2/14 T.M.B.

2449 Wt. W14957/M90 750,000 1/16 J.B.C. & A. Forms/C.2118/12.

Vol 6

War Diary for

August 1916

43rd Trench Mortar Battery

43rd Trench Mortar Battery

Instructions regarding War Diaries and Intelligence Summaries are contained in F. S. Regs., Part II. and the Staff Manual respectively. Title Pages will be prepared in manuscript.

WAR DIARY
or
~~INTELLIGENCE SUMMARY~~
(Erase heading not required.)

14th Division

Army Form C. 2118.

Place	Date	Hour	Summary of Events and Information	Remarks and references to Appendices
Field	1.8.16		The battery marched from Remaisnil to Le Meillard where they remained for six days. The time was employed by training the men in the gun ~~& [illegible]~~ & getting the men fit.	[initials]
"	7.8.16		The battery marched from Le Meillard to Candas to entrain. They disentrained at Rebemont & marched into camp near Albert.	[initials]
"	8.8.16 to 11.8.16		Time was spent in training the battery in the advance	[initials]
"	12.8.16		The battery went into action on this day. Two guns were put in Longueval & two guns in Delville Wood.	[initials]
	16.8.16		I was ordered to put eight guns into action so as to be able to fire on certain points of the enemies lines to help in an attack which was carried out on the 18th inst	[initials]
	17.8.16		The day was spent in finding & building the eight emplacements.	
	18.8.16		The whole of the battery moved up into action at 6. pm with orders to keep up a slow fire during the day untill five	

2449 Wt. W14957/M90 750,000 1/16 J.B.C. & A. Forms/C.2118/12.

43rd Trench Mortar Battery. 14th Division

Instructions regarding War Diaries and Intelligence Summaries are contained in F. S. Regs., Part II. and the Staff Manual respectively. Title Pages will be prepared in manuscript.

WAR DIARY
or
~~INTELLIGENCE SUMMARY~~
(Erase heading not required.)

Army Form C. 2118.

Place	Date	Hour	Summary of Events and Information	Remarks and references to Appendices
Field	1.8.16		The battery marched from Remaisnil to Le Meillard where they remained for six days. The time was employed by training the men in the gun ~~[illegible]~~ & getting the men fit.	[illegible]
"	7.8.16		The battery marched from Le Meillard to Candas to entrain. They disentrained at Rebemont & marched into camp near Albert.	[illegible]
"	8.8.16 – 11.8.16		Time was spent in training the battery in the advance.	[illegible]
"	12.8.16		The battery went into action on this day. Two guns were put in Lon[illegible] & two guns in Delville Wood.	[illegible]
	[illegible].8.16		I was ordered to put eight guns into action so as to be able to fire on certain points of the enemies lines to help in an attack which was carried out on the 18th inst.	[illegible]
	17.8.16		The day was spent in finding & building the eight emplacements.	
	18.8.16		The whole of the battery moved up into action at 6 pm with orders to keep up a slow fire during the day until five	

2449 Wt. W14957/M90 750,000 1/16 J.B.C. & A. Forms/C.2118/12.

Army Form C. 2118.

Instructions regarding War Diaries and Intelligence Summaries are contained in F. S. Regs., Part II. and the Staff Manual respectively. Title Pages will be prepared in manuscript.

WAR DIARY
~~or~~
~~INTELLIGENCE SUMMARY~~

(Erase heading not required.)

2

Place	Date	Hour	Summary of Events and Information	Remarks and references to Appendices
Field	18.8.16		minutes before Zero. Five minutes before Zero rapid fire was ordered.	
			In the evening ~~the~~ two of the guns were ordered to help in a bombing attack which was to be carried out by the 6th K.O.Y.L.I. The bombing attack was not carried out. A shell fell into one of the position blowing up the ammunition & killing 2/Lieut Morrish & wounding one man. The gun was destroyed	[illegible]
	19.8.16		The battery was relieved by the 41st Trench mortar Battery. On the relief being complete the battery marched back to Pommiers Redoubt where they remained the night marching on to Fricourt camp the following morning where the remained till the 25th.	[illegible]
	25.8.16		On the night of the 25th inst the battery moved up to Delville Wood & took up four positions.	[illegible]
	27.8.16		Two guns fired about 50 rounds in a portion of the enemies trenches called Ale Alley	[illegible]

Instructions regarding War Diaries and Intelligence Summaries are contained in F. S. Regs., Part II. and the Staff Manual respectively. Title Pages will be prepared in manuscript.

WAR DIARY
~~or~~
~~INTELLIGENCE SUMMARY~~

(Erase heading not required.)

Army Form C. 2118.

Place	Date	Hour	Summary of Events and Information	Remarks and references to Appendices
Field	18-8-16		minutes before Zero. Five minutes before Zero rapid fire was ordered.	
		"	In the evening the two of the guns were ordered to help in a bombing attack which was to be carried out by the 6th K.O.Y.L.I. The bombing attack was not carried out. A shell fell into one of the position blowing up the ammunition & killing 1 Sergt [illegible] & wounding one man. The gun was destroyed.	[illegible]
	19-8-16		The battery was relieved by the 41st Trench Mortar Battery. On the relief being completed the battery marched back to Pommiers Redoubt where they remained the night marching on to Fricourt camp the following morning where the remained till the 25th.	[illegible]
	25-8-16		On the night of the 25th inst the battery moved up to Delville Wood & took up four positions.	[illegible]
	27-8-16		Two guns fired about 50 rounds in a portion of the enemies trenches called Ale Alley	[illegible]

2449 Wt. W14957/M90 750,000 1/16 J.B.C. & A. Forms/C.2118/12.

Army Form C. 2118.

Instructions regarding War Diaries and Intelligence Summaries are contained in F. S. Regs., Part II. and the Staff Manual respectively. Title Pages will be prepared in manuscript.

~~WAR DIARY~~ ~~or~~ INTELLIGENCE SUMMARY

(Erase heading not required.)

3

Place	Date	Hour	Summary of Events and Information	Remarks and references to Appendices
Field	29.5.16		Four positions were dug in the new front line to assist in a bombing enterprise but the guns were not required	J.W.C.
"	30.5.16		On the night of the 30/31st the battery was relieved & marched to Fricourt. As half the battery was not relieved until the morning of the 31st they were taken on lorries from Fricourt to Hornoy. The remainder of the battery proceeded there by train.	J.W.C.
			J.W. [illegible] Clarke Capt. O.C. 43rd T.M. Batt.	

2449 Wt. W14957/M90 750,000 1/16 J.B.C. & A. Forms/C.2118/12.

Instructions regarding War Diaries and Intelligence Summaries are contained in F. S. Regs., Part II. and the Staff Manual respectively. Title Pages will be prepared in manuscript.

WAR DIARY
or
INTELLIGENCE SUMMARY

(Erase heading not required.)

3

Army Form C. 2118.

Place	Date	Hour	Summary of Events and Information	Remarks and references to Appendices
Field [?]	29.8.16 [?]		Four positions were dug in the new front line to assist in a bombing enterprise but the guns were never required	[illegible]
"	30.8.16 [?]		On the night of the 30/31st the battery was relieved & marched to F[illegible]recourt. As half the battery was not relieved until the morning of the 31st they were taken on lorries from F[illegible]recourt to Hornoy. The remainder of the battery proceeded there by train.	[illegible]

[illegible] Clarke Capt.
O.C. 43rd T.M. Bty

Vol 2

C O N F I D E N T I A L

W A R D I A R Y

O F

HEAVY TRENCH MORTAR BATTERY, 14TH DIVISION

From August 1st. To August 31st

(VOLUME 11)

Instructions regarding War Diaries and Intelligence Summaries are contained in F. S. Regs., Part II. and the Staff Manual respectively. Title Pages will be prepared in manuscript.

Army Form C. 2118

WAR DIARY
or
~~INTELLIGENCE~~ SUMMARY
(Erase heading not required.)

1

August.

V/14 HEAVY TRENCH MORTAR BATTERY.
No.
Date 31 · 8 · 16.

Place	Date	Hour	Summary of Events and Information	Remarks and references to Appendices
ARRAS	1		Battery at rest in billets in ARRAS.	
	2		" " " " " " "	
	3		" " " " " " "	
	4		Battery proceeds to billets in LUCHEUX	
	5		" " " " " BERNAVILLE. Lt. E.G.F. GUNNING appointed Temp^y. Captn.	
	6		Battery at rest in billets in BERNAVILLE.	
	7		Battery proceeds to billets in VILLERS - BOCAGE	
	8		" " " " " BUIRE Sheet 62^D E. 13. c. central	
E. 13. c. central	9 to 11		Battery at rest in billets in " " " "	
	12		Battery proceeds to billets Sheet 62^D. E. 10. c. central.	
E. 10. c. central	13		Battery at rest in billets " " " "	
	14		" " " " " " " " "	
	15		" " " " " " " " "	
	16		" " " " " " " " "	
	17		" " " " " " " " "	
	18		" " " " " " " " "	
	19		" " " " " " " " "	

1875 Wt. W593/826 1,000,000 4/15 J.B.C. & A. A.D.S.S./Forms/C. 2118.

Instructions regarding War Diaries and Intelligence Summaries are contained in F. S. Regs., Part II. and the Staff Manual respectively. Title Pages will be prepared in manuscript.

Army Form C. 2118

2 WAR DIARY or ~~INTELLIGENCE SUMMARY~~

(Erase heading not required.)

August.

Place	Date	Hour	Summary of Events and Information	Remarks and references to Appendices
Sheet 62D E.10.c. central	20		Battery at rest in billets Sheet 62D E.10.c. central. Battery takes over 4 guns (one damaged) from V/14 Heavy Trench Mortar Battery. One gun being taken over in position, the remaining three, including the one damaged, taken over in rest area. Gun taken over in position remaining there in rest.	
	21		Battery at rest in billets Sheet 62D. E.10.c. central. Gun in position at rest.	
	22		" " " " " " " " " " " " "	
	23		" " " " " " " " " " " " "	
	24		Gun in position fires on New trench running from S.11.a.2.3 through S.11.b.0.5½ in accordance with 14th D.A. O.O. No 38 dated 23.8.16. Area in vicinity of gun shelled by Germans after firing, gun being buried in 3 feet of earth at 9 pm. Remainder of battery in rest at E.10.c. central.	

1875 Wt. W593/826 1,000,000 4/15 J.B.C. & A. A.D.S.S./Forms/C. 2118.

Instructions regarding War Diaries and Intelligence Summaries are contained in F. S. Regs., Part II. and the Staff Manual respectively. Title Pages will be prepared in manuscript.

3

WAR DIARY
or
~~INTELLIGENCE SUMMARY~~

(Erase heading not required.)

August.

V/14 HEAVY TRENCH MORTAR BATTERY.
No. ....
Date 31.8.16.

Army Form C. 2118

Place	Date	Hour	Summary of Events and Information	Remarks and references to Appendices
Sheet 62D E.10.c. Central	25		Debris cleared away from gun in position. Gun undamaged.	
			Battery at rest in E.10.c. central. Gun in position at rest.	
	26		" " " " " " " " " "	
	27		" " " " " " Gun in position again buried by shell fire.	
	28		" " " " " " Gun in position at rest, undamaged	
	29		" " " " " " " " " "	
	30		" " " " " " Gun in position again buried by shell fire	
E.11.c.5.7	31		Battery proceeds to billets E.11.c.5.7. Gun in position at rest, undamaged.	

E B Jennings
Captain R.G.A.
Comdg. V/14 Heavy T.M. Bty.

1875 Wt. W593/826 1,000,000 4/15 J.B.C. & A. A.D.S.S./Forms/C. 2118.

ORIGINAL.

Vol 6

C O N F I D E N T I A L

W A R   D I A R Y

O F

T R E N C H   M O R T A R   B A T T E R I E S

F O R

S E P T E M B E R   1 9 1 6

(VOLUME 111)

Instructions regarding War Diaries and Intelligence Summaries are contained in F. S. Regs., Part II. and the Staff Manual respectively. Title Pages will be prepared in manuscript.

WAR DIARY
or
~~INTELLIGENCE SUMMARY~~
(Erase heading not required.)

September.

V/14 HEAVY TRENCH MORTAR BATTERY.
No. 1
Date.

Army Form C. 2118

Place	Date	Hour	Summary of Events and Information	Remarks and references to Appendices
Sheet 62D E.11.C.5.7	1		One quarter personnel of Battery attached 14th Div R.A. Signals as runners ~~in~~ during forthcoming operations. One Subsection with gun in action in MACGREGOR TRENCH. Remainder of Bty at rest in E.11.C.5.7	
	2		" " " " " " " " "	
	3		" " " " " " " " "	
			2Lt. A. H. S. TAYLOR R.F.A having been dismissed the Service by Sentence of F.G.C.M leaves for England.	
	4		One quarter personnel of Battery attached R.A Signals as runners, One Subsection with gun in action in MACGREGOR TRENCH, Remainder of Battery at rest in E.11.C.5.7	
	5 6 7 8 9		" " " " " "	

1875 Wt. W593/826 1,000,000 4/15 J.B.C. & A. A.D.S.S./Forms/C. 2118.

Instructions regarding War Diaries and Intelligence Summaries are contained in F. S. Regs., Part II. and the Staff Manual respectively. Title Pages will be prepared in manuscript.

WAR DIARY

or

~~INTELLIGENCE SUMMARY~~

(Erase heading not required.)

September

V/14 HEAVY TRENCH MORTAR BATTERY.

No. 2

Date.

Army Form C. 2118

Place	Date	Hour	Summary of Events and Information	Remarks and references to Appendices
Sheet 62D E.11.c 5.7	10		2 Guns taken into position at S.10.c.9.4 in order to take part in 14th D.A. Operation order No 47 dated 11.9.16.	
	11		One Subsection with gun in MACGREGOR TRENCH, remainder of Battery with 2 guns at S.10.c.9.4	
	12 13 14 15 16		" " " " " " " "	
	17		Gun in MACGREGOR TRENCH withdrawn to X Roads S.16.a.3.9 having been completely buried. Other 2 guns remaining with detachments at S.10.c.9.4.	
	18		2 Guns in action at S.10.c.9.4	
	19 20 21 22 23 24 25 26 27		" " " " " "	

1875 Wt. W593/826 1,000,000 4/15 J.B.C. & A. A.D.S.S./Forms/C. 2118.

Instructions regarding War Diaries and Intelligence Summaries are contained in F. S. Regs., Part II. and the Staff Manual respectively. Title Pages will be prepared in manuscript.

WAR DIARY
or
INTELLIGENCE SUMMARY
(Erase heading not required.)

September

V/14 HEAVY TRENCH MORTAR BATTERY.
No. 3
Date.

Army Form C. 2118

Place	Date	Hour	Summary of Events and Information	Remarks and references to Appendices
Sheet 62D E.11.C.5.7	28		2 Guns in position at S.10.C.9.4 and Gun at X Roads S.16.a.3.9 withdrawn. Battery at rest in E.11.C 5 7. less men employed as runners.	
	29		Battery less men employed as runners at rest in E.11.C.5.7.	
	30		" " " " " " " " " "	

[signature]
Captain R.F.A.
Comdg V/14 Heavy T.M. Batty.

1875 Wt. W593/826 1,000,000 4/15 J.B.C. & A. A.D.S.S./Forms/C. 2118.

Instructions regarding War Diaries and Intelligence Summaries are contained in F. S. Regs., Part II. and the Staff Manual respectively. Title Pages will be prepared in manuscript.

WAR DIARY
or
~~INTELLIGENCE~~ SUMMARY
(Erase heading not required.)

Army Form C. 2118.

September 1st – 30th 1916

X/14 Trench Mortar Battery.

Place	Date	Hour	Summary of Events and Information	Remarks and references to Appendices
E. 11. Central	1st	2pm	Moved Camp from E10 C 4.2 To E. 11. Central	MAP REF. Sheet No 62 D NE.
"	3	8AM	X/14 By relieved Z/14 By in Carlton Terrace.	Map ref. Sheet No 57c S.W
	4 5 and 6		Digging Gun Emplacements in Black Watch Trench at S. 10. b 4.3. Emplacements Completed.	
	7	3pm	Relieved by Z/14 By.	
	8		2/Lt. J.G. WALSER attached to Y/14 By as temp O.C.	
	12	10AM	Medium Batteries relieved by New Zealand T. M. B'ys. After this period the usual Daily Parades were carried out	
	13.	–	2/Lt. J. G. WALSER awarded the Military Cross.	
	15.		Battery Personnel helping at Corps Dressing Station.	
	18	–	Battery Personnel digging O. P. for the 46 Bde. R.F.A	
	19 – 30		Usual Parades & Inspections Carried out.	

H B Davis

Lt. R.F.A O/C X/14 T.M. By.

2449 Wt. W14957/M90 750,000 1/16 J.B.C. & A. Forms/C.2118/12.

Map ref: Sheets 57 + 62.

Instructions regarding War Diaries and Intelligence Summaries are contained in F. S. Regs., Part II. and the Staff Manual respectively. Title Pages will be prepared in manuscript.

WAR DIARY

or

~~INTELLIGENCE SUMMARY~~

(Erase heading not required.)

Army Form C. 2118.

Place	Date	Hour	Summary of Events and Information	Remarks and references to Appendices
Near ALBERT E11C central	1-9-16.		Moved camp from E10C central to E11C. central where men were accomodated in bivouacks.	
S10b27.	5-9-16.		2/Lt: E.G. Porter + half battery went up to Black Watch trench + made 4 positions with aid of R.E.	
	6-9-16.		~~4pos~~ Work continued on Black Watch positions.	
	7-9-16.		Lieut C.C.O. Taylor relieved Lieut. H.B. Davis. The Four positions in Black Watch completed to cover Tea Trench + Wood Lane.	
	8-9-16.		2/Lt: E.G. Porter + half battery relieved by other half of 2/14 Battery. Owing to infantry succeeding in taking Tea Trench + Wood Lane the guns in Black Watch were not required to fire.	
	10-9-16.		Guns in Black Watch taken out of action.	
	12-9-16		Lieut: Taylor + half battery relieved by X Battery New Zealand T.M.	
F7C central	17-9-16.		Battery on fatigue duty at XV th Corps dressing station BECORDEL.	
	18-9-16			
S10C33.	19-9-16.		Battery sent to 47th Bde. R.F.A. Headqrs: for fatigue duty.	
F7C. central	20-9-16 to 21-9-16.		Battery continued fatigue duties at XV Corps dressing station BECORDEL.	

C. C. O. Taylor Lieut.

Cmdg: 2/14 T.M.B.

2449 Wt. W14957/M90 750,000 1/16 J.B.C. & A. Forms/C.2118/12.

Vol #7

Confidential

War Diaries

of

14th Divisional Trench Mortar Batteries.

From Oct 1st To October 31st 1916.

Instructions regarding War Diaries and Intelligence Summaries are contained in F. S. Regs., Part II. and the Staff Manual respectively. Title Pages will be prepared in manuscript.

WAR DIARY ~~or INTELLIGENCE SUMMARY~~

(Erase heading not required.)

X/14 T.M.By.

October 1st – 31st 1916.

Army Form C. 2118.

Place	Date	Hour	Summary of Events and Information	Remarks and references to Appendices
E.11.c. Central	2	8AM	Marched to BONNAY. Billets. Rained.	Map ref Sheet 62D NE FRANCE.
BONNAY	3.	2PM.	" " MOLLIENS do do	
MOLLIENS	4	1.30PM	" " AUTHIEULE do do	
AUTHIEULE	5	10AM	Motor Lorries to LATTRE ST QUENTIN. Billets. Rained.	LENS 11.
LATTRE ST QUENTIN	6	5PM	do do " WAILLY. Action. Billets. Relieved X/12 T.M.By. 9pm.	FRANCE 51C S.E.
R.21 D 10.1.	8	4PM	Registered Nos 1 & 2 Guns Enemy's Sap at R34 b 5.7 and front line at R.34 b 10.85.	FICHEUX 51B S.W.
do	9	4.2AM	Fired 65 Rounds in Conjunction with 46 Division Operation Orders, with Nos 1 & 2 Guns onto Enemy's front line at R34 b 5.8 to R34 b 10.85 between 4.2 & 4.35 A.M.	
do	10	—	Registered No. 3 gun onto Enemy's Sap at R.35 a 2.85.	
do	12	3PM	Relief took place. Retaliated for Enemy's Minenwerfers; which were successfully silenced.	
do	13	—	Registered D Sap at R30 a ½.9.	
do	15	-	do C. Sap at R29 b 84.61. Enemy retaliated with Vane Bombs, 77MM & 4.2s.	
do	16	-	do G1 Sap at M19 a 3.7 No retaliation.	
do	17.	-	Commenced wire Cutting. Orders from 41/F.B. Considerable wire was cut by our mortars at R29 D 1½.6 to R29 D 3.7 and trenches badly damaged. Enemy did not retaliate.	
do	18	2AM	Relief Took place. A most successful Shoot was carried out on Enemy's wire at R34 b 90.85 and at R34 b 83.85. The Gaps in the Enemy's wire were considerably widened by our fire.	
do	19	—	Orders received from 41/F.B. Cancelling wire cutting.	
do	20	—	New Gun Emplacement dug at FERRET St opposite C. Sap.	

Army Form C. 2118.

Instructions regarding War Diaries and Intelligence Summaries are contained in F. S. Regs., Part II. and the Staff Manual respectively. Title Pages will be prepared in manuscript.

WAR DIARY
or
~~INTELLIGENCE SUMMARY~~

(Erase heading not required.)

X/14 T. M. By.
October 1st – 31st 1916.

Place	Date	Hour	Summary of Events and Information	Remarks and references to Appendices
R21D10.1.	21	–	Registered C Sap at R29 & 89.61 from new position in FERRET St.	Map ref Sheet No. 51B S.W. FICHEUX
do	23	10 AM	Cpl NEARY Granted leave. Retaliated for Minenwerfers.	
do	24	2 pm	Relief took place	
do	25th		Repairing Dug Outs & Gun Emplacements.	
			41/I.B. relieved by B Division 37/I.B	
do	26		Visited Battalion & Company Commanders.	
do	27		Selected new positions with D.O.T.M. for Special Shoot arranged by VI Corps.	
do	28		Retaliated for Small T. Ms. Preparing position for Corps Shoot.	
do	29		Positions for Corps Shoot Completed.	
do.	30	2 pm.	Relief Took place	

H.B. Davis
O.C. X/14 T.M.By.

2449 Wt. W14957/M90 750,000 1/16 J.B.C. & A. Forms/C.2118/12.

Instructions regarding War Diaries and Intelligence Summaries are contained in F. S. Regs., Part II. and the Staff Manual respectively. Title Pages will be prepared in manuscript.

Army Form C. 2118.

WAR DIARY
or
~~INTELLIGENCE SUMMARY~~
(Erase heading not required.)

Y/14 T.M.B^y 14th DIVISION

Place	Date	Hour	Summary of Events and Information	Remarks and references to Appendices
Meaulte.	1/10/16	–	LT E G PORTER took over Y/14 T.M.B. from LT E.H. FLETCHER who was transferred to Home Service.	
BONNAY	2/10/16		Battery left Meaulte for BONNAY. where billets were found for the night.	
MOLLIENS. AUTHIEULLE	3rd–4th		Moved on to Molliens & then Authieulle & next day to Lattre St Quentin.	
LATTRE St QUENTIN	6th		Left Lattre St Quentin by lorry for trench billet at AGNY. Took over from Y/12 Trench Mortar Battery at night in J sector with 3 guns.	
AGNY.	7 Oct		Hostile trench mortaring about 4 pm. We retaliated & enemy ceased	
"	8 Oct		LT AIKEN went on leave. Fired in retaliation for mortars.	
"	9–10		Quiet. No firing.	
"	11		Fired in retaliation to enemy's minenwerfers.	
"	12–16		Quiet. Finished off emplacement which 12th DIVISION had started.	
"	17.		Were ordered to cut wire M15. a. 8 0. M14. d. 1.1 M20 a 7.9. to M20. a. 5.7. Map ref. 41 rounds fired. Good effect	NEUVILLE VITASSE. 51B. SW.1.
"	18.		110 rounds fired at above mentioned points. A fair amount of wire was cut.	
"	19.		Wire cutting cancelled by B.G.C 42nd I.B.	
"	20.		Quiet. LT AIKEN returned from leave.	
"	21		24 rounds fired in retaliation	
"	22		23 rounds fired.	
"	23–29.		Enemy's mortars very quiet only 37 rounds fired between 23rd & 29th.	
"	30		Quiet.	
"	31.			

2449 Wt. W14957/M90 750,000 1/16 J.B.C. & A. Forms/C.2118/12.

No. of rounds fired 255 month ending 31/10/16.

E G Porter Lieut.
O.C. Y/14 T.M.B.

Army Form C. 2118.

Instructions regarding War Diaries and Intelligence Summaries are contained in F. S. Regs., Part II. and the Staff Manual respectively. Title Pages will be prepared in manuscript.

WAR DIARY ~~or~~ ~~INTELLIGENCE SUMMARY~~

(Erase heading not required.)

Place	Date	Hour	Summary of Events and Information	Remarks and references to Appendices
MEAULTE Nr ALBERT	2-10-16		Battery struck camp at MEAULTE + marched to billets at BONNAY.	
	3-10-16		Battery left BONNAY + marched to billets in MOLLIENS.	
	4-10-16		Battery left MOLLIENS + marched to huts in AUTHIEULE.	
	5-10-16		Battery left AUTHIEULE by motor lorry for billets in LATTRE ST QUENTIN.	
	6-10-16		Battery left LATTRE ST QUENTIN by motor lorry + proceeded to ARRAS to	
ARRAS.			relieve Z/12 T.M.B. Six guns were taken to trenches that evening.	
	7-10-16		Guns mounted at M4b17, M4b76, M4b86, G35C13, G35C56, G35C75.	
	9-10-16		Fired 5 rounds to register M4b76. 2/Lieut C.M.SAMUEL posted to Z/14 T.M.B from 14 D.A.	
	10-10-16		Lieut: C.C.O.TAYLOR proceeded to 3rd Army T.M. School for 8 days course.	
	12-10-16		Orders received to prepare six guns for wire cutting.	
	13-10-16		Fired 139 rounds at wire + enemy trenches.	
	14-10-16		Fired 13 rounds in retaliation.	
	17-10-16 to 23-10-16		Fired 911 rounds at wire + trenches causing 3 complete gaps in enemy wire.	
	24-10-16		New targets for wire cutting started. Fired 70 rounds.	
	25-10-16 to 26-10-16		Fired ~~7~~ 156 rounds at enemy wire + trenches	

2449 Wt. W14957/M90 750,000 1/16 J.B.C. & A. Forms/C.2118/12.

Instructions regarding War Diaries and Intelligence Summaries are contained in F. S. Regs., Part II. and the Staff Manual respectively. Title Pages will be prepared in manuscript.

WAR DIARY

~~or~~

~~INTELLIGENCE SUMMARY~~

(Erase heading not required.)

Army Form C. 2118.

Place	Date	Hour	Summary of Events and Information	Remarks and references to Appendices
ARRAS.	27-10-16		2/Lt: C. M. SAMUEL proceeded to England on 10 days leave. Battery fired 85 rounds at trenches & wire.	
	28-10-16 to 30-10-16.		Fired 187 rounds at wire & trenches.	
	31-10-16.		Orders received to suspend wire cutting operations.	

[illegible]
Lieut.
O.C. Z/14 T.M.B.
31-10-16.

2449 Wt. W14957/M90 750,000 1/16 J.B.C. & A. Forms/C.2118/12.

Instructions regarding War Diaries and Intelligence Summaries are contained in F. S. Regs., Part II. and the Staff Manual respectively. Title Pages will be prepared in manuscript.

WAR DIARY or INTELLIGENCE SUMMARY

(Erase heading not required.)

October.

V/14 HEAVY TRENCH MORTAR BATTERY. No. 4/1 Date.

Army Form C. 2118

IV Volume.

Place	Date	Hour	Summary of Events and Information	Remarks and references to Appendices
Sheet 62D E.11.c.5.7	1		Guns handed over to N.Z. Trench Mortar Batty. Men employed as runners with F.A. Brigades return to Battery.	
	2		Battery proceeds to billets at BONNAY	
	3		" " " " " MOULIENS-AU-BOIS	
	4		" " " " " AUTHIEULLE	
	5		" " " " " LATTRE-ST-QUENTIN	
L.35.c.2.7	6		" " " " " DAINVILLE. 2 guns taken over from V/12 Heavy Trench Mortar Batty - Guns in position at M.4.c.80.93 and M.14.c.03.32. Detachments with guns, remainder of Battery in billets at L.35.c.2.7.	
	7 8 9 10 11		Working parties finishing emplacement at M.14.c.03.32. Telephone System completed.	
	12		30 Torpedoes received ready for operations on 13th. Gun moved from M.14.c.03.32 to position dug during the day at M.9.b.95.80	

1875 Wt. W593/826 1,000,000 4/15 J.B.C. & A. A.D.S.S./Forms/C. 2118.

Instructions regarding War Diaries and Intelligence Summaries are contained in F. S. Regs., Part II. and the Staff Manual respectively. Title Pages will be prepared in manuscript.

October

WAR DIARY or INTELLIGENCE SUMMARY

(Erase heading not required.)

V/14 HEAVY TRENCH MORTAR BATTERY.
No. 4/2
Date.

Army Form C. 2118

Place	Date	Hour	Summary of Events and Information	Remarks and references to Appendices
L.35.c.2.7	13		In conjunction with O.O. 62 of 46th Bde. R.F.A. Battery bombarded enemy's dugouts at M.10.d.6.7½., firing 28 torpedoes between 4 pm and 6 pm. 8 direct hits on target, remainder of rounds in enemy's trench in front of same.	
	14 15 16 17 18 19 20		Dug-outs build at L.35.c.2.7 for accomodation. Detatchments with 2 guns in action, remainder of Battery working on dug-outs at L.35.c.2.7.	
	21		Gun moved from emplacement at M.9.b.95.80 to original position at M.14.c.03.32. 80 torpedoes received ready for Operations on 22nd. Torpedoes dumped at Groupe des Maisons. 2Lt. E.F. MELLOR. R.F.A. joins the Batty on being posted from A/47 Bde R.F.A.	
	22		Operations postponed until 23rd. 35 Torpedoes carried from Groupe des Maisons to position at M.14.c.03.32.	
	23		~~Operation~~ Unfavaurable weather conditions prevent Operations being	

1875 Wt. W593/826 1,000,000 4/15 J.B.C. & A. A.D.S.S./Forms/C. 2118.

Instructions regarding War Diaries and Intelligence Summaries are contained in F. S. Regs., Part II. and the Staff Manual respectively. Title Pages will be prepared in manuscript.

WAR DIARY
or
INTELLIGENCE SUMMARY
(Erase heading not required.)

V/14
HEAVY TRENCH
MORTAR BATTERY.
No. 4/3
Date.........

Army Form C. 2118

Place	Date	Hour	Summary of Events and Information	Remarks and references to Appendices
L.35.c.2.7	23		Carried out according to time table pre-arranged. The shoot which was timed to commence at 9am, started at 1pm when better conditions prevailed. 35 rounds were fired on M.11.a.2.5 M.11.a.1.5 to M.10.b.8.2 M.11.a.1.5 to M.10.b.6.8 and supposed T.M. emplacement at M.4.d.7.4 The shoot was very successful. Enemy trench system severely damaged.	
	24		Damage to emplacement caused by concussion of gun in firing on 23rd rebuilt.	
	25 26 27 28 29 30 31		Working parties, day and night, completing gun emplacement in HAYMARKET TRENCH.	

[signature]
Captn R.F.A.
Comdg V/14 Heavy T.M. Bty.

1875 Wt. W593/826 1,000,000 4/15 J.B.C. & A. A.D.S.S./Forms/C. 2118.

Vol 8

C O N F I D E N T I A L

W A R D I A R Y

O F

14TH DIVISIONAL TRENCH MORTAR BATTERIES.
(Mediums & Heavy)

From 1st November 1916. To 30th November 1916

Army Form C. 2118.

WAR DIARY
or
~~INTELLIGENCE SUMMARY~~

(Erase heading not required.)

Instructions regarding War Diaries and Intelligence Summaries are contained in F. S. Regs., Part II. and the Staff Manual respectively. Title Pages will be prepared in manuscript.

X/14 Trench Mortar Bty.

November 1st – 30th 1916.

Place	Date	Hour	Summary of Events and Information	Remarks and references to Appendices
Wailly	1st to 4th		All Quiet	Map ref. 51c S.E. & 51 B S.W.
	5	2pm	Relief took place	
	[illegible]-11		Repairing positions damaged by Rain.	
	11	2pm	Relief took place	
	12		Preparing position in FRIARY St covering Z15 Enemy Sap.	
	14	7pm	Handed over to 2/Lt WALSER whilst acting D.T.M.O.	
	15	—	Retaliated with two Guns for Enemy Organised Shoot on left Battalion front line firing 80 rounds. Fired 46 rounds onto Z15 Sap. Completely laid the Head of Sap open, destroying much wire.	
	17	–	At request of Infantry fired 60 rounds onto Enemy's new work in front line at R.34 b 4.8½	
	18		Fired 15 rounds in retaliation for Enemy Minenwerfers; onto Sap Z10, destroying much wire.	
	19		Fired 66 rounds onto Sap Z9A, two Gaps being Cut in wire.	
	20		Retaliated for Enemy H.T.M. with two guns firing 30 rounds onto Z15 and 31 rounds at Enemy H.T.M. at R.30 a 4.4. Effectively silencing Enemy Mortar.	
	21		Fired onto Enemy working party at R34 b 4.8; successfully dispersing same.	
	22		Fired 9 rounds only onto Z14 Sap; Mechanisms of two guns were blown out.	
	23		Retaliated for Enemy H.T.M. onto his front line at R.29. d 3.6½.	
	23		Battery Sergeant & Gunner wounded by Enemy Small T.M. Bomb.	
			Battery Sergeant died from wounds received on the 23rd inst.	
	24		Retaliated onto Enemy front line for H.T.M.	
	25 & 26		Fired onto Enemy's new work at R34 b 6.7½, many direct hits were obtained on his trench & much water was thrown up.	
	27		Retaliated onto Enemy Support line at R34 b 7.7	
	28		Retaliated on Enemy Minenwerfer at R35 a ½.6 which had been seen firing the day previous.	
	29		Fired 38 rounds onto Z15 Sap destroying most of the wire at Head of Sap – Several direct hits were obtained on Sap. Took Battery over from 2/Lt WALSER.	
	30		Total number of rounds fired for month ending 30/11/16. 633 Rounds.	

H B Davis Lt. RFA
O.C. X/14 T.M.B.

Army Form C. 2118.

Instructions regarding War Diaries and Intelligence Summaries are contained in F. S. Regs., Part II. and the Staff Manual respectively. Title Pages will be prepared in manuscript.

WAR DIARY
~~or~~
~~INTELLIGENCE SUMMARY~~
(~~Erase heading not required.~~)

Y/14 T.M. Bty   14th Division

Place	Date	Hour	Summary of Events and Information	Remarks and references to Appendices
~~[illegible]~~ Field	1/1/16	—	3 Mortars in action in J. sector. Fired 15 rounds.	
	4/1/16.		Fired 65 rounds, ordinary retaliation	
	5 to 11/16			
	6–7.		Cutting wire M20 a 5.8 (Ref Sheet Map NEUVILLE.VITASSE ~~[illegible]~~ 57B SW1) 93 rounds fired	
	8–27		normal average retaliation fire. 309 rounds fired during this period.	
	28.	2pm to 4pm	2 hour bombardment of enemys line about M 15 c ~~[illegible]~~ 5 in conjunction with 18 pounders 4.5 Hows & 6 inch ~~Hows~~. 2 mortars firing for an hour, fired 82 rounds	
	29		Fired 3 rounds	
	30.		Preparations for a raid, wire cutting about M20 a 5.8 – 6.9. & M14 c 2 5 Fired 65 rounds	

E.G. Porter
Lieut
O/c Y/14 T.M.B.

2449 Wt. W14957/M90 750,000 1/16 J.B.C. & A. Forms/C.2118/12.

Instructions regarding War Diaries and Intelligence Summaries are contained in F. S. Regs., Part II. and the Staff Manual respectively. Title Pages will be prepared in manuscript.

WAR DIARY
~~or~~
~~INTELLIGENCE SUMMARY~~
(Erase heading not required.)

Z/14 Trench Mortar Battery

Army Form C. 2118.

Place	Date	Hour	Summary of Events and Information	Remarks and references to Appendices
ARRAS.	1-11-16 to 19-11-16.		628 Rounds were fired in first 19 days of month against Enemy Machine Gun positions, Observation Posts, Trench Tramways & T.M. positions. An enemy Medium T.M. at M5a65 was put out of action by two direct hits on 15-11-16 & has not fired since.	
	20-11-16.		38 Rounds fired in arranged shoot with Stokes T.M. on MAISON ISOLEE M10b46.	
	21-11-16.		Very misty day no observation possible. 20 Rounds fired on registered targets.	
	22-11-16 & 23-11-16.		81 Rounds fired in conjunction with Stokes & 9.45" T.M. on M5a78 & M4d63 & M10b46. Enemy T.M. retaliated & succeeded in burying one gun after firing 60 Rounds at it. 2/Lieut. C. M. SAMUEL on leave ordered a Medical Board in England. 2/Lieut. G. W. JONES posted to Z/14 T.M.B.	
	24-11-16.		20 Rounds fired for registration on M4b81.	

2449 Wt. W14957/M90 750,000 1/16 J.B.C. & A. Forms/C.2118/12.

Instructions regarding War Diaries and Intelligence Summaries are contained in F. S. Regs., Part II. and the Staff Manual respectively. Title Pages will be prepared in manuscript.

WAR DIARY

~~or~~

~~INTELLIGENCE~~ SUMMARY ~~Z/14 T.M.B.~~ Z/14 T.M.B.

(Erase heading not required.)

Army Form C. 2118.

Place	Date	Hour	Summary of Events and Information	Remarks and references to Appendices
ARRAS.	25-11-16.		50 Rounds fired in arranged shoot with Stokes T.M. against M4d62.	
	26-11-16.	2pm	33 Rounds fired against M5a78 in arranged shoot with Stokes T.M.	
		4.30pm	36 Rounds fired in conjunction with 14th D.A. + VI Corps H.A. against enemy tramway line M10b69 to M4d71.	
	27-11-16.		5 Rounds fired at G35d30 to register gun.	
	28-11-16 to 30-11-16		267 Rounds fired at enemy wire at M4d57, M4b92 + M5a88.	
			Total Number of Rounds fired during month 1178.	
		Map	51B.	
			C. C. O. Taylor Lieut. O.C. Z/14 T.M.B.	

2449 Wt. W14957/M90 750,000 1/16 J.B.C. & A. Forms/C.2118/12.

Instructions regarding War Diaries and Intelligence Summaries are contained in F. S. Regs., Part II. and the Staff Manual respectively. Title Pages will be prepared in manuscript.

WAR DIARY
or
INTELLIGENCE SUMMARY
(Erase heading not required.)

Army Form C. 2118

V/14 HEAVY TRENCH MORTAR BATTERY. No. 1 Date 5/1

November.

Place	Date	Hour	Summary of Events and Information	Remarks and references to Appendices
L.35.c.27.	1st to 10th		2 Guns in action in HAVANAH TRENCH and GATE STREET	
	11		Capt. E.G.F. GUNNING having joined 3rd Army School of Mortars as Instructor is struck off the strength. Lt E.W. LOWE R.F.A takes over Command of Battery. 2Lt. H.E. WALLER joins Battery on being posted from D/46 Bde. R.F.A.	
	12 to 19		2 Guns in action in HAVANAH TRENCH and GATE STREET	
	20		Pre-arranged Bombardment of MAISON ISOLEE. M.10.b.37.68 The shoot was very successful, several direct hits being observed.	
	22		Working parties detatched for building of Divl. O.P's.	
	23		Lt E.W. LOWE R.F.A. proceeds on leave to ENGLAND. 2Lt H.E. WALLER R.F.A takes over Command of Battery.	
	25		Bombardment of Enemy T.M. emplacement at M.10.b.77. Seven good bursts around target observed.	
	26		Bombardment of Tram Line M.10.b.63.87. Reported very effective.	
	27 30		1 Gun received from 3rd Army School of Mortars.	

E.J. Mellor 2/Lt. R.F.A.
for Comdg V/14 H.T.M. Batty.

1875 Wt. W593/826 1,000,000 4/15 J.B.C. & A. A.D.S.S./Forms/C. 2118.

819

WAR DIARY.

of

TRENCH MORTAR BATTERIES 14TH DIVN.

From 1st December 1916. To 31st December 1916.

( )

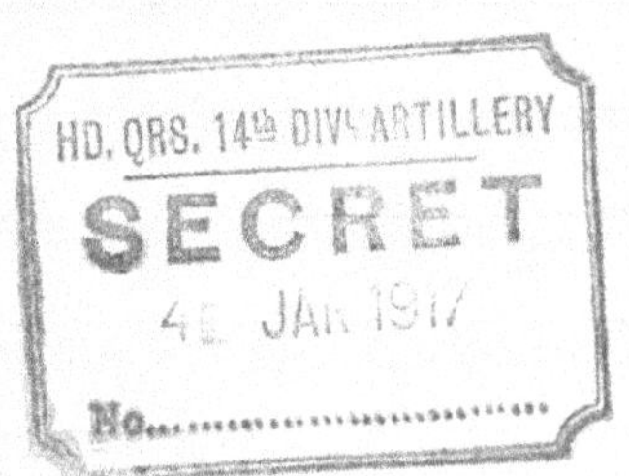

Instructions regarding War Diaries and Intelligence Summaries are contained in F. S. Regs., Part II. and the Staff Manual respectively. Title Pages will be prepared in manuscript.

WAR DIARY

or

~~INTELLIGENCE SUMMARY~~

(Erase heading not required.)

Army Form C. 2118.

X/14 Trench Mortar Bty.
December 1st – 31st 1916.

Place	Date	Hour	Summary of Events and Information	Remarks and references to Appendices
WAILLY	2nd	–	Received Operation Orders from 37 I.B. No 107.	
"	2	8 P.M.	X/12 Medium Trench Mortar Bty. arrived with 4 Guns to reinforce and operate in conjunction with 37 I.B. O.O. No 107.	
"	3	10 AM	Wire Cutting commenced. Fired 182 rounds.	
"	4	9 " "	" " " 402 " The Enemy retaliated with Heavy Minenwerfers, doing much damage to our trenches.	
"	5	10 AM	Wire Cutting fired 290 rounds.	
"	6	10.30 AM	" " " 254 " Reports received from Battalion Commanders state:- that wire round & connecting Z14 & Z15 Saps was completely destroyed.	
"	7	6 P.M.	Relieved by & handed over to X/12 T.M.By. Motor Transport to Rest Billets at IVERGNY.	
IVERGNY	8th–31st		Usual parades & Inspections carried out daily.	

H.B. Davis
Lt. R.F.A.
O.C. X/14 T.M. Bty.

2449 Wt. W14957/M90 750,000 1/16 J.B.C. & A. Forms/C.2118/12.

Instructions regarding War Diaries and Intelligence Summaries are contained in F. S. Regs., Part II. and the Staff Manual respectively. Title Pages will be prepared in manuscript.

WAR DIARY
or
~~INTELLIGENCE SUMMARY~~

(Erase heading not required.)

Y/14 T.M.B.

Army Form C. 2118.

Place	Date	Hour	Summary of Events and Information	Remarks and references to Appendices
'C' Sector Map 51B SW1	1/12/16 to 7/12/16		No special operations were carried. Normal retaliatory firing daily – 169 rounds were fired.	
NEUVILLE VITASSE	7-12-16	7pm	The battery was relieved by Y/12 TMB & removed to rest area IVERGNY	
	8/12/16 to 29/12/16		Rest area. Deficiencies in kit made up & gun stores checked & completed. Usual course of training daily including physical drill, marching, anti-gas drill & testing of box respirators.	
	29/12/16		1 gun & crew temporarily attached Z/14 by & proceeds into action 'H' sector Map 51B.SW.1 NEUVILLE VITASSE 1/10000	
	30/12/16 31/12/16		Training continues.	

[signature] Capt
O.C. TMB

2449 Wt. W14957/M90 750,000 1/16 J.B.C. & A. Forms/C.2118/12.

Instructions regarding War Diaries and Intelligence Summaries are contained in F. S. Regs., Part II. and the Staff Manual respectively. Title Pages will be prepared in manuscript.

WAR DIARY

or

~~INTELLIGENCE SUMMARY~~

(Erase heading not required.)

Army Form C. 2118.

Z/14 T.M.B

Place	Date	Hour	Summary of Events and Information	Remarks and references to Appendices
ARRAS	1/12/16		Wire cutting continued in accordance with orders from 35th I. Bde.	
[illegible]			117 rounds were fired with good effect, at M4d5.7. M4d5.9. M4b9.2.	
51B. SW1	2/12/16	"	Firing continued on points indicated above 131 rounds fired.	
(NEUVILLE-	3/12/16	12.30pm	150 rounds fired at same objectives.	
VITASSE)			One gun position at G35.c.2½ was blown in burying One Officer & 4 other ranks. After 2½ hours digging 2 O.R's were extricated alive, no sign of the ~~[illegible]~~ Officer or O.R's until 24 hours later when they were dug out dead. The officer was the O.C. Battery Lieut C.C.O. TAYLOR	
'H' Sector.	4/12/16 to 7/12/16		Firing continued throughout ~~the~~ these days cutting wire at same points 275 rounds being fired	
	7/12/16	8pm	Relieved by Z/12 & withdrew guns personnel to rest area IVERGNY	
	8/12/16		2Lt T.G. WALSER is transferred from X/14 T.M.B & takes over command of Bty.	
	8/12/16 to 29/12/16		Deficiencies of kit & gun stores made up, & all ranks start course of training (physical drill, marching & [illegible] gun drill) which continues daily throughout rest period.	
	29/12/16	3/30am	Bty goes into action 'H' Sector to reinforce Z/12 T.M.B for special operation, with one gun detached from X/14 & one from Y/14. T.M.B	
	30/12/16 31/12/16		Work on temporary gun positions & registration of 6 guns, 101 rounds fired.	

2449 Wt. W14957/M90 750,000 1/16 J.B.C. & A. Forms/C.2118/12.

[signature] Capt.
D.T.M. 14 Divn.

Instructions regarding War Diaries and Intelligence Summaries are contained in F. S. Regs., Part II. and the Staff Manual respectively. Title Pages will be prepared in manuscript.

WAR DIARY
or
INTELLIGENCE SUMMARY
(Erase heading not required.)

December.

V/14 HEAVY TRENCH MORTAR BATTERY. No. 6/1 Date 31-12-16.

Army Form C. 2118

Place	Date	Hour	Summary of Events and Information	Remarks and references to Appendices
DAINVILLE L.35.c.2.7	1		2 Guns in action in HAVANAH TRENCH and GATE STREET	
	2		Pre-arranged shoot on enemy's front line about M.20.a.5.3.	
	3		Bombardment of enemy's trenches M.5.C.20.05. M.10.b.7.7. M.11.a.2.7 and M.11.a.3.0. 38 rounds fired. Several direct hits on enemy dug-outs observed.	
	4		Special registration of gun in GATE STREET on enemy's trenches M.20.c.3.9 to M.20.a.9.4.	
	5		Enemy sap at M.5.a.8.5. bombarded at request of Infantry. Shoot reported very effective.	
	6		Pre-arranged shoot on enemy reserve line between M.20.c.7.9 and M.20.d.2.3	
IVERGNY.	7		Battery proceeds to Rest Billets at IVERGNY	
	8		Captn E.W. LOWE R.F.A. returns from leave to England, takes over Command of Battery.	
	9 to 30		Battery in rest Billets at IVERGNY.	

E.W. Lowe. Captn RFA
Comdg V/14 Hvy T.M. Batty.

1875 Wt. W593/826 1,000,000 4/15 J.B.C. & A. A.D.S.S./Forms/C. 2118.

Vol 10

C O N F I D E N T I A L

W A R D I A R Y

of

X, Y, Z, Medium Trench Mortar Batteries.

From - January 1st, 1917. To - January 31st, 1917.

Volume

==*=*=*=*=*=*=*

Instructions regarding War Diaries and Intelligence Summaries are contained in F. S. Regs., Part II. and the Staff Manual respectively. Title Pages will be prepared in manuscript.

WAR DIARY
or
~~INTELLIGENCE SUMMARY~~

(Erase heading not required.)

Army Form C. 2118.

X/14 T. M. By.
January 1st – 31st 1917.

Place	Date	Hour	Summary of Events and Information	Remarks and references to Appendices
IVERGNY.	1–7	—	Rest Billets.	
"	8	2 pm	Motor transport from IVERGNY to WAILLY; where we relieved the X/12 T. M. By in "F" Sector at 8 pm. Relief clear. Billet, Bombstores, Dug Out and Material	
WAILLY	8		left in very bad condition.	
"	12	–	Re-registered all Guns.	
"	15		R.Es digging. Seven (7) new Gun pits & Shelters.	
"	18	.	Infantry Carrying parties filling up Bombstores 125 rounds per Gun	
"	26		" " " Completed carrying up 2000 rounds.	
"	30		Enemy Heavy Minenwerfers very active, destroying 300 yards of our front line wire.	
"	31		Counter Offensive	

H B Davis
Lt. RFA.

2449 Wt. W14957/M90 750,000 1/16 J.B.C. & A. Forms/C.2118/12.

Instructions regarding War Diaries and Intelligence Summaries are contained in F. S. Regs., Part II. and the Staff Manual respectively. Title Pages will be prepared in manuscript.

Army Form C. 2118.

WAR DIARY
or
INTELLIGENCE SUMMARY for JANUARY.

(Erase heading not required.)

Place	Date	Hour	Summary of Events and Information	Remarks and references to Appendices
	7th/8th		Relieved Y/12 on the night of 7th 8th Jan at AGNY.	
	8th to 15th		This weeks work was on, (a) Laying telephone lines between guns & repairing wire from guns to Hdqs. (b) Repairing wooden frame for Newton beds in the line, Hostile fire during week very little. We fired 19 rounds.	
	16th to 23rd		Several new points registered i.e. Communication trenchs, Saps etc. Combined Artillery & T.M. shoot on Saps Y3, Y4, Y5. on 19th Jan we fired 44 rounds on these saps, with good results, Hostile fire during week about normal, we fired 79 rounds. during the week.	
	24th to 30th		New standings & roofing for bomb store made. Position & approaches to Gravel St emplacement repaired Wire laid to two new O.P.s	
		26th	Combined Artillery & TM shoot on enemy front line at M15c 3653 and from M15c 0025, to M15c 1530. We fired 34 rounds. Enemy retaliated to the left of Railway but was silenced,	
		30th	At 7.5am enemy started severe T.M. bombardment on our front line from G1 to G6 & behind front line at G14 to G16. we retaliated & after a while silenced him we fired 46 rounds, The bombardment which evidently was an organised shoot was intense, & was silenced about 9 am.	
Night	30th/31st		Relieved by 2/30 TMB. Rounds fired from 8th to 30th Jan, 223 Rounds	
	31st		Out at Arrass.	

Y/14 MEDIUM TRENCH MORTAR BATTERY. No. J.C.31 Date 31-1-17.

J Cranmer Lt R.F.A.
O.C. Y/14 T.M.B.

2449 Wt. W14957/M90 750,000 1/16 J.B.C. & A. Forms/C.2118/12.

Instructions regarding War Diaries and Intelligence Summaries are contained in F. S. Regs., Part II. and the Staff Manual respectively. Title Pages will be prepared in manuscript.

WAR DIARY
or
~~INTELLIGENCE SUMMARY~~

(Erase heading not required.)

Army Form C. 2118.

Z/14 T.M. Battery

Place	Date	Hour	Summary of Events and Information	Remarks and references to Appendices
ARRAS	8.1.17		This battery took over H Sector from Z/12 TMB. Previous to that this battery came into action on 29/12/16 to help the 12 Division in a special operation on 6.1.17 firing 400 rounds.	
	8/1/17 to 22/1/17		Ordinary retaliation. 4 guns in action. Two old positions improved and one new one in Keltar Street started. New telephone wires laid to all guns and O.P.'s.	
	23/1/17		Organised Shoots on enemy front line M 4 d 6.1. to 7.5 Three guns shooting. 150 rounds fired during the afternoon.	
	26/1/17		94 rounds fired from two guns into enemy H.T.M. tramway at M 4 d 7 3 in conjunction with our Heavy T.M.	
			On the same day two guns were put into temporary positions on the left of sector in Hunter St & Hulluch. Ground terribly hard digging nearly impossible. Both guns registered on 26/1/17.	
	27/1/17		Five guns now in action. Much trouble on account of rifle mechanism continually going wrong.	
	28/1/17		54 rounds fired into enemy T.M. emplacements (in retaliation) M4d 8.3	
	29/1/17		24 rounds fired into enemy lines in Beaurains (retaliation)	
	30/1/17		94 rounds fired. Bombardment of enemy trenches on the left of Hunter St, & retaliation on Birchfields.	
	31/1/17		194 rounds fired [illegible] organised bombardment in conjunction with Artillery on the left of Hunter St. & retaliation on to Beaurains	J.M. Clemow [illegible] Lieut RFA Z/14 T.M. Batt

2449 Wt. W14957/M90 750,000 1/16 J.B.C. & A. Forms/C.2118/12.

C O N F I D E N T I A L

W A R D I A R Y

of

V/14 Heavy Trench Mortar Battery.

From - January 1st, 1917. To - January 31st, 1917.

Volume

==*=*=*=*=*=*=*

Instructions regarding War Diaries and Intelligence Summaries are contained in F. S. Regs., Part II. and the Staff Manual respectively. Title Pages will be prepared in manuscript.

WAR DIARY
or
~~INTELLIGENCE SUMMARY~~
(Erase heading not required.)

January 1917.

Army Form C. 2118

V/14 HEAVY TRENCH MORTAR BATTERY. No. 7/1 Date.

Place	Date	Hour	Summary of Events and Information	Remarks and references to Appendices
IVERGNY	1		Battery in rest Billets at IVERGNY.	
	2		" " " " " "	
	3		" " " " " "	
	4		" " " " " " 2Lt. J. THOMSON-EVANS R.F.A. joins Battery on being posted from C/46 Bde. R.F.A.	
	5		" " " " " "	
	6		" " " " " "	
	7		" " " " " "	
DAINVILLE	8		Battery proceeds to DAINVILLE relieving V/12 Hvy T.M. Batty, taking over 4 guns in the line at HUNTER ST - HAVANNAH - HAYMARKET and GATE STREET. 2Lt. H. E. WALLER R.F.A. leaves the Battery to join 35th D.A. on being posted there.	
	9 to 18		4 guns in action. HAVANNAH and HAYMARKET positions repaired.	
	19		Pre-organised bombardment of enemy T.M. emplacement at M.5.b.75.75.	
	20		Gun in GATE STREET moved to emplacement at FLOOD STREET	
	21		Gun emplacement at HAYMARKET blown in by enemy's fire burying gun.	

1875 Wt. W593/826 1,000,000 4/15 J.B.C. & A. A.D.S.S./Forms/C. 2118.

Instructions regarding War Diaries and Intelligence Summaries are contained in F. S. Regs., Part II. and the Staff Manual respectively. Title Pages will be prepared in manuscript.

WAR DIARY
or
INTELLIGENCE SUMMARY
(Erase heading not required.)

V/14 HEAVY TRENCH MORTAR BATTERY. No. 7/2 Date.

Army Form C. 2118

Place	Date	Hour	Summary of Events and Information	Remarks and references to Appendices
DAINVILLE	22		Shoot on enemy trenches between M.10.b.5.9 and 5.6	
	24		Gun in HUNTER STREET moved to emplacement in FRENCH ST.	
	26		Bombardment of enemy T.M. emplacements in vicinity of M.4.d.75.15 and M.10.b.7.7	
	30		Shoot on M.10.b.9.4 at request of Infantry in retaliation for enemy T.M. fire. Bombardment of enemy trench mortar emplacement at R.29.d.85.85. Rounds were observed to fall in close vicinity of target.	

E. W. Lml. Capt. R.F.A.
Comdg V/14 H.T.M. Bty.

1875 Wt. W593/826 1,000,000 4/15 J.B.C. & A. A.D.S.S./Forms/C. 2118.

Vol XI

C O N F I D E N T I A L

W A R   D I A R Y .

O F

X, Y, & Z/14 MEDIUM TRENCH MORTAR BATTERIES.

From 1st February, 1917 to 28th February, 1917.

Volume

Army Form C. 2118.

Instructions regarding War Diaries and Intelligence Summaries are contained in F. S. Regs., Part II. and the Staff Manual respectively. Title Pages will be prepared in manuscript.

WAR DIARY
or
INTELLIGENCE SUMMARY
(Erase heading not required.)

Place	Date FEB	Hour	Summary of Events and Information	Remarks and references to Appendices
NAILLY	1.		FOREST ST. NO 1. gun position badly damaged by 4.2 cm. shell & entrance to dugout.	
	2.		Only 1 gun in action - mechanisms all broken.	
	3.		Handed ammunition over to D.T.M.O 49 Div. - Rounds on hand 1864. Rounds in reserve 631. - Enemy shelled shrine next to billet with 77mm shells	
	4.	6p.m.	TOOK 49th D.T.M.O. over our positions in F Sector. X/14 bty comes under G.O.C. 49 Div at 6 p.m. 3/2/17	
	6.		Fired 6 rds. in retaliation	
	7.		Gun in action at FRENCH ST	
	8.		LIEUT H. B. DAVIS admitted to hospital suffering from trench fever. He hands over to 2LT. A.M. DOUGLASS	
	9.		LIEUT. A.A.V. HOATHER is appointed from 1ST ROYAL BERKS. to be D.T.M.O. 14 DIV vice A/CAPT. J.W. CAMERON, M.C. who is appointed C.T.M.O. VII Corps	
	10.		Fired 3 rounds in retaliation	
	13.		10 5.9 cm. shells into billet - but no damage.	
	14		Fired 6 rounds in retaliation	
	17.		2LT. W. S. POPE joins the battery from D/47 R.F.A.	
		10 p.m. to 10.30 p.m.	Fired 35 rds from 3 guns in connection with a raid (O.O. 68) successfully carried out by 4 DUKE OF WELLINGTON'S REGT - 49 W.R. DIV when 1 prisoner of the 392 Inf. Regt 46 (2 SAXON) RES. BDE.	

2449 Wt W14957/M90 750,000 1/16 J.B.C. & A. Forms/C.2118/12.

Instructions regarding War Diaries and Intelligence Summaries are contained in F. S. Regs., Part II. and the Staff Manual respectively. Title Pages will be prepared in manuscript.

WAR DIARY
or
INTELLIGENCE SUMMARY
(Erase heading not required.)

Army Form C. 2118.

2

Place	Date	Hour	Summary of Events and Information	Remarks and references to Appendices
VAILLY	18.		Commenced wire-cutting (D.T.M.O. O.O 34) in connection with 147 I.B. (O.O. 69) in conjunction with 2 guns 49 DIV. when 68 rds. were fired	
	19.		Continued wire cutting - 80 rds. being fired when O.O. 69 was cancelled	
	20.		Fired 4 rds. in retaliation	
	21		" 29 " " . Enemy T.M's now very active throughout the sector. Had 1 direct hit on exit to FRENCH ST. dugout, completely blocking it & 2 vane bombs into gun pit. - no casualties.	
	22.		Fired 24 rds. in retaliation. Put gun into FOREST ST. Trouble with mechanisms wh. are very hard to replace.	
	23.		Fired 18 rds. in retaliation. Enemy T.M's now much quieter. V/49 H.T.M. BTY. now in action with 1 gun in FLOOD ST. - Brewery Dump shelled with salvos of 4.2 shells - no damage.	
	24.		4 guns in action viz - FOREST, FLAG, FRENCH & FLEET STS.	
	26.		Fired 12 rds. at request of Inf. in retaliation to vane bombs	
	27.		Fired 7 rounds in retaliation.	

A. M. Douglas [illegible] 2nd Lt. R.F.A.
O.C. X/14 T.M. Bty.
28/2/17

2440 Wt. W1495/M90 750,000 1/16 J.B.C. & A. Forms/C.2118/12.

Army Form C. 2118.

Instructions regarding War Diaries and Intelligence Summaries are contained in F. S. Regs., Part II. and the Staff Manual respectively. Title Pages will be prepared in manuscript.

WAR DIARY
or
INTELLIGENCE SUMMARY of Y/14 T.M. Battery.

(Erase heading not required.)

Place	Date	Hour	Summary of Events and Information	Remarks and references to Appendices
Arras	1-2-17 to 10-2-17		Battery out of the line. Men employed on Fatigues etc. All men were Inoculated during this period.	
	11-2-17 to 28-2-17		Making 4 gun Battery position at G 35d 5884 This position is nearly completed with the exception of ammunition slip trenches.	

J P Crammer 2Lt R.F.A.
O.C. Y/14 T.M. Battery

28. 2-17

2449 Wt. W14957/M90 750,000 1/16 J.B.C. & A. Forms/C.2118/12.

Army Form C. 2118.

Instructions regarding War Diaries and Intelligence Summaries are contained in F. S. Regs., Part II. and the Staff Manual respectively. Title Pages will be prepared in manuscript.

WAR DIARY
of
~~INTELLIGENCE SUMMARY~~ Z/14 T.M.Bty

(Erase heading not required.)

Place	Date	Hour	Summary of Events and Information	Remarks and references to Appendices
Arras	1		Registered Sap x 12 with B 3 and front line M 4 d 50,95 to M 4 d 5,6 with 4 H – 90 rounds fired	
	2		40 rounds fired in retaliation	
	3 & 4		nothing fired	
	5	5.30pm	Enemy's Hvy Trench Mortars fired in neighbourhood of Havannah at 5.30pm Guns 3 A & 4 A replied with 41 rounds	
	6		nothing fired	
	7		All quiet during day – Few 4.2's at 6.30 pm.	
	8		Quiet day 15 rounds fired in retaliation	
	9		5 rounds fired in retaliation on G.35 d 8.3.	
	10		Rounds fired nil Very Quiet day	
	11		" " " " " "	
	12		" " " " " "	
	13	2.45 pm	Fired 8 rounds 3 A & 3 B. Observed from Haymarket. Target front line & beyond. no retaliation	
	14		Fired 8 rounds 3 A, 3 B 4 A no retaliation	
	15		11 rounds upon front line. No reply. C.O. Ox & Bucks wishes for no unnecessary firing	
	16		Rounds fired nil	
	17		do	
	18		Rounds fired 4 on M 4 d 50 62 checking registration	
	19		" " 5 on G 35 95 checking registration	

2449 Wt. W14957/M90 750,000 1/16 J.B.C. & A. Forms/C.2118/12.

Army Form C. 2118.

Instructions regarding War Diaries and Intelligence Summaries are contained in F. S. Regs., Part II. and the Staff Manual respectively. Title Pages will be prepared in manuscript.

WAR DIARY of ~~INTELLIGENCE SUMMARY~~ X/14 T.M. Bty.

(Erase heading not required.)

Place	Date	Hour	Summary of Events and Information	Remarks and references to Appendices
Arras	20		Fired nil	
	21		Five rounds were fired by 4 b. no retaliation	
	22		Six rounds were fired by 3 b upon target M 4 d 7 2 (Tramway). Last two rounds were very short owing to trouble with mechanism blowing out & burning thread.	
	23	noon	Enemy dropped 5 medium mortars near Ronville - Beaurains Road without doing damage. Following this were a dozen bombs. We retaliated with 12 rounds from 3 A and 8 rounds from 3 b. Afternoon & evening quiet. N.B. Reappearance of Heavy Trench Mortars opposite "H". They came from Right of Beaurains, i.e. South-East.	
	2		We fired about 56 rounds in retaliation for enemy's heavy trench mortars – and their medium mortars firing from between Havannah & Hamilton and Buckfields.	
	25		Rounds fired about 60 from 3 A & 3 b. 3 A emplacement has been knocked in. 3 b. BED has crumpled up and broken rear clamp.	
	26		nothing fired up to noon. Rebuilding 3 b. emplacement. Strafe in "G" Sector 9 am. New bed brought up to 3 b which comes into action again. Bed fetched from Helsas St. to 4 A which also came into action. no Enemy ~~hvy~~ trench mortars.	
	27		4 A & 4 b. Ready for wire cutting. nothing fired. No enemy's mortars.	
	28		Telephone connected to O.P. in "N" Support Line. Registered 4 A & 4 b & started wire cutting. Fired 40 rounds upon wire M 5 a 05,15. Very lively artillery fire on left (10 pm). Clouds of smoke observed behind enemy's lines. Red & Green Rockets up.	

J. W. Lemon
2/Lieut. R.F.A.
for O.C. X/14 T.M. Bty.

2449 Wt. W14957/M90 750,000 1/16 J.B.C. & A. Forms/C.2118/12.

C O N F I D E N T I A L.

W A R   D I A R Y .

O F .

V/14 HEAVY TRENCH MORTAR BATTERY.

From 1st February, 1917 to 28th February, 1917.

Volume.

WAR DIARY
or
INTELLIGENCE SUMMARY
(Erase heading not required.)

Army Form C. 2118.

V/14 HEAVY TRENCH MORTAR BATTERY.
No. 8/1
Date.

Instructions regarding War Diaries and Intelligence Summaries are contained in F. S. Regs., Part II. and the Staff Manual respectively. Title Pages will be prepared in manuscript.

February.

Place	Date	Hour	Summary of Events and Information	Remarks and references to Appendices
DAINVILLE L.35.c.2.7	1st		10 rounds were fired on M.10.b.9.0 in retaliation at request of Infantry. 4 Guns in the line.	
	3rd	nightly	Working Party salving gun etc which was blown in at Haymarket pit on 21.?.17	
	4th		〃 〃 〃	
			Gun in "F Sector in FLOOD ST handed over to 49th Hvy T.M. Batty.	
			" " F sector in FRENCH ST removed & put into position in H Sector in HUNTER ST.	
	5th		Gun received from 49th Div. Trench Mortars	
	To	nightly	Working party working on HAYMARKET PIT.	
	7th	"	〃 〃 〃	
ARRAS G.27.b.6.0	night 9th/10th		Battery vacated billets at DAINVILLE L.35.c.2.7 & proceeded to billets in ARRAS at G.27.b.6.0.	
	12th to 28th	daily	Working parties employed on new Heavy Trench Mortar Positions in H. Sector	

E. W. Lowe
Capt R.F.A.
Comdg V/14 Hvy T.M. Batty.

2449 Wt. W14957/M90 750,000 1/16 J.B.C. & A. Forms/C.2118/12.

Vol 12

C O N F I D E N T INA L.

W A R   D I A R Y

O F

14th Divisional Trench Mortar Batteries,

From 1st March, 1917 to - March 31st, 1917.

Instructions regarding War Diaries and Intelligence Summaries are contained in F. S. Regs., Part II. and the Staff Manual respectively. Title Pages will be prepared in manuscript.

WAR DIARY
or
INTELLIGENCE SUMMARY
(Erase heading not required.)

Army Form C. 2118.

X/14 T.M. Battery
14 Div.
MARCH 1917

Place	Date	Hour	Summary of Events and Information	Remarks and references to Appendices
WAILLY	2		Orders to withdraw from F. Sector.	
"	3	9.15 P.M	Withdraw from F. Sector & proceed to ARRAS. Battery billeted in house 16 RUE EMILE LENGLET.	
ARRAS	4-19		Attached to 2/14 T.M. for fatigues, work &c on positions in H. SECTOR.	
"	20		Enemy withdraw on our front & batteries withdrawn, as we are now out of range.	
"	20-25		Work on forward ammunition dump at M 4 b 5.6	
"	26-29		Attached to 62nd Field Coy. R.E. building tramlines & also carrying parties	
"	31		Attached to 14 R.A. Signals burying wires.	

X/14 MEDIUM TRENCH MORTAR BATTERY. No. .... Date 31/3/17

[illegible]
O.C. X/14 T.M.B.

2449 Wt. W14957/M90 750,000 1/16 J.B.C. & A. Forms/C.2118/12.

Army Form C. 2118.

Instructions regarding War Diaries and Intelligence Summaries are contained in F. S. Regs., Part II. and the Staff Manual respectively. Title Pages will be prepared in manuscript.

WAR DIARY
or
INTELLIGENCE SUMMARY

(*Erase heading not required.*)

Y/14 TMBty for March 1917

Place	Date	Hour	Summary of Events and Information	Remarks and references to Appendices
1·3·17	1st		Preparing gun positions to cut wire from M5a9085 to G35d5813	
	2nd		Commenced firing 2 men wounded, ~~Fired~~	
	2nd to 11th		2nd inst to 11th inst fired 1394 Rounds on wire between above map references	
ARRAS	12th to 17th		12th inst to 17th inst fired 246 Rounds on wire between G35d9056 & G35d7530	
	18th		Enemy retreated from "Beaurains"	
	19th to 24th		19th inst to 24th inst carrying bombs from positions rendered out of Range by enemy retiring	
	25 to 27		25th inst to 27th inst supplied working parties to 62nd Coy R.E.	
	28th to 30th		28th inst to 30th inst Transporting Bombs.	
	31st		Supplied working party to R. A. Signal Officer for digging Cable trench	

J Cranmer Lt RFA.
O.C. Y/14 T.M.B.

2449 Wt. W14957/M90 750,000 1/16 J.B.C. & A. Forms/C.2118/12.

Army Form C. 2118.

Instructions regarding War Diaries and Intelligence Summaries are contained in F. S. Regs., Part II. and the Staff Manual respectively. Title Pages will be prepared in manuscript.

WAR DIARY ~~or~~ 2/14 T. M. Bty.
~~INTELLIGENCE SUMMARY~~

(*Erase heading not required.*)

Place	Date	Hour	Summary of Events and Information	Remarks and references to Appendices
Field	Mar 1		Wire cutting continued with 4 A & 4 B on M 5 a 00.14 to M 5 a 15.25 good results were obtained with very little retaliation. 150 rounds were fired	On 4 Mar at 7.30 pm Gnr Frame & Gnr [illegible], owing to the number of duds went out voluntarily to the enemy's wire and brought back six 60 lb bombs, making in all three [illegible] enemy's. Owing to their act of conspicuous gallantry, the new fuze cap was able to be carefully examined, the [illegible] in the ammunition. These six bombs were disguised and fired again into the enemy's wire with good effect. On March 10 put in a recommendation for the D.C.M. for these 2 men. On March 14 they were awarded the military medal.
	2		Wire cutting continued with same guns. Gap widened and cut through. A few "whiz bangs" were fired at the two positions. 140 rounds fired.	
	3		Wire cutting continued. Little retaliation. 155 rounds fired.	
	4		Gap in wire widened M 4 b 95.15 to M 5 a 16.26 and 136 rounds fired. There was a high percentage of "duds" which was probably due to the new cap on the newton fuze. Enemy retaliated at 4 pm with a few 4.2's	
	5		Wire cutting with same two guns. 182 rounds fired and very good results obtained. Remainder of wire "nil". Enemy retaliated most of the afternoon with small Minnenwerfer hitting 4 B position with one and wounding Gnr Dedlock. Several more "duds". Smoke seen rising from Brick-fields	
	6		Wire cutting continued and gap widened to the right to M 4 b 9 1 with 4 A gun. 158 rounds fired and no retaliation. 18 pdrs cutting just to right.	
	7		Wire cutting on left of Bank at M 5 a 2 4 commenced and further right of M 4 b 9 1. Few whiz bangs in retaliation	
	8		Fired 118 rounds on wire at same place as on 7th inst. Shelled out of O. P. Yorkshires had 2 men killed and 4 wounded just in trench by O. P.	

2449 Wt. W14957/M90 750,000 1/16 J.B.C. & A. Forms/C.2118/12.

Instructions regarding War Diaries and Intelligence Summaries are contained in F. S. Regs., Part II. and the Staff Manual respectively. Title Pages will be prepared in manuscript.

Army Form C. 2118.

WAR DIARY of Z/14 T.M. Bty (cont)

~~INTELLIGENCE SUMMARY~~

(Erase heading not required.)

Place	Date	Hour	Summary of Events and Information	Remarks and references to Appendices
Field	Mar. 9		Fired 201 rounds wire cutting and 12 rounds registering flanks of entrant.	
	10		Raid postponed Fired 3 rds from 3 B in registration of new wire	
	11		Wire cutting continued with same two guns. 98 rds fired and good results were obtained 65 fired into Sap X 19 30 into Saps 16 to 18 and 3 from 3 A for registration	
	12		110 rounds fired during raid in co-operation with the Artillery There were no "Duds" and a good line was kept.	
	13		Rounds fired nil	
	14		do	
	15		One gun placed in Holborn - Helsas position and wire cutting commenced at M 5 a 6.8. 40 rounds fired	
	16		Another gun put in above position for wire cutting at M 5 a 5.7 100 rds fired and a lane partially cut. No new wire has been observed at Saps X 16 to X 19. Very little retaliation	
	17		Wire cutting was continued from Helsas - Holborn position on M 5 a 4.6 M 5 a 5 7 and a lane cut through 100 rds were fired with no retaliation.	
	18		Rounds fired nil Enemy apparently retiring all along the line	
	19		Rounds fired nil Enemy retired from F G & H Sectors Our patrols in Beaurains.	
	20		Rounds fired nil Started carrying bombs from 4 A & 4 B to Hamilton Position our Forward Dump	

2449 Wt. W14957/M90 750,000 1/16 J.B.C. & A. Forms/C.2118/12.

Army Form C. 2118.

Instructions regarding War Diaries and Intelligence Summaries are contained in F. S. Regs., Part II. and the Staff Manual respectively. Title Pages will be prepared in manuscript.

WAR DIARY
of Z/14 T.M. Bty (contd)
~~INTELLIGENCE SUMMARY~~
(Erase heading not required.)

Place	Date	Hour	Summary of Events and Information	Remarks and references to Appendices
Field	Mar 21		Bomb carrying continued and slit trenches covered	
	22		Bomb carrying from 4A & 4B finished. All beds taken out and brought down from the line	
	23		Bomb carrying commenced from Helsas - Holborn position to Forward Dump. Pieces etc brought down from the line.	
	24		Bomb carrying continued from Helsas Holborn Position	
	25		Battery attached to 62nd Field Coy RE for work. Bomb carrying finished. Six 2" T.M. beds sent to I.O.M. VII Corps to be fitted with Arcs & pointers.	
	26		—	
	27		—	
	28		All ammunition and component parts checked (4,900 rounds) to be handed over.	
	29		—	
	30		—	
	31		Battery attached to RA Signals for work (1 officer & 40 men)	

G. D. Jones. Lieut RGA
O.C. Z/14 T.M. Bty.

2449 Wt. W14957/M90 750,000 1/16 J.B.C. & A. Forms/C.2118/12.

Confidential

War Diary

for

Trench Mortars

X. V. Y. & Z. Batteries

1st April to 30th 1917

Volume 24

Instructions regarding War Diaries and Intelligence Summaries are contained in F. S. Regs., Part II. and the Staff Manual respectively. Title Pages will be prepared in manuscript.

WAR DIARY
or
INTELLIGENCE SUMMARY

(Erase heading not required.)

Army Form C. 2118.

X/14 T.M. BTY. APRIL

Place	Date	Hour	Summary of Events and Information	Remarks and references to Appendices
ARRAS	1-5		Attached to R.A. Signals digging cable trenches	
SIMENCOURT	6-16		H.Q. & X, Y, Z batteries except guards, & signallers who are attached to 46 Army F.A. (ARRAS) ~~[illegible]~~ at SIMENCOURT.	
ARRAS	17-20		Batteries attached to 46 & 47 F.A. ~~Rde~~ Bde salvaging ammunition	
	18		H.Q. & remainder of batteries return to ARRAS.	
WANCOURT	21		Cpl. [illegible] killed, Gr. [illegible] died of wounds, & Gr. [illegible] wounded whilst attached to 46 F.A. Bde	
ARRAS	25-30		Signallers attached to R.A. & batteries working parties under 46 F.A. Bde.	

[illegible signature]
O.C. X/14

2449 Wt. W14957/M90 750,000 1/16 J.B.C. & A. Forms/C.2118/12.

Instructions regarding War Diaries and Intelligence Summaries are contained in F. S. Regs., Part II. and the Staff Manual respectively. Title Pages will be prepared in manuscript.

WAR DIARY
or
INTELLIGENCE SUMMARY
(Erase heading not required.)

Army Form C. 2118.

X/14 T.M. BTY. APRIL '1

Place	Date	Hour	Summary of Events and Information	Remarks and references to Appendices
ARRAS	1-5		Attached to R.A. Signals digging cable trenches.	
SIMENCOURT	6-16		H.Q. & X, Y, Z Batteries except guards & signallers who are attached to 48 Army F.A. (ARRAS) remove to SIMENCOURT.	
ARRAS	17-20		Batteries attached to HQ 47 F.A. Bde. taking ammunition.	
–	18		H.Q. & remainder of batteries return to ARRAS.	
W[illegible]NCOURT	21		Cpl. [illegible] killed, Gr. Darvill died of wounds, & Gr. Thompson wounded whilst attached to 46 F.A. Bde.	
ARRAS	25-30		Signallers attached to R.A. & batteries on working parties under 46 F.A. Bde.	

[illegible signature]
O.C. X/14

2449 Wt. W14957/M90 750,000 1/16 J.B.C. & A. Forms/C.2118/12.

Army Form C. 2118.

Instructions regarding War Diaries and Intelligence Summaries are contained in F. S. Regs., Part II. and the Staff Manual respectively. Title Pages will be prepared in manuscript.

WAR DIARY
of X/14 T. M. Bty
~~INTELLIGENCE SUMMARY~~
(Erase heading not required.)

Place	Date	Hour	Summary of Events and Information	Remarks and references to Appendices
Arras.	April 1-5		Provided working party for F.A. Signals digging cable trench from BRICKFIELDS to NAPPER TRENCH	
	4		1 Officer 2 telephonists and 1 servant attached to 48th Army F.A. Bde 2/Lt J. N. Elmore evacuated	
	night 5-6		Battery less guards and working party proceed to SIMENCOURT	
Simencourt	6		Working party rejoin from Arras.	
	7-16		Resting at SIMENCOURT. Marching Drill and football	
	16		Party return from 48 Army F.A. Bde.	
	17		Provide working party of 15 O.R's who proceed to RONVILLE working for 50th D.A.	
	18		Proceeded to ARRAS	
Arras	19 to 24		Training at ARRAS.	
	25		1 Officer, 2 telephonists and 1 servant attached to 48 Army F.A. Bde for Liaison Duty	
	26-28		Training continued	
	29		Major Hudson Commandant Third Army School of Mortars inspects Mortars including a captured "Minenwerfer (Med)"	
	30		Battery attached to Divisional Artillery digging Gun Positions near WANCOURT.	

W. Pope Lt
OC
X/14 T. M. Bty.

2449 Wt. W14957/M90 750,000 1/16 J.B.C. & A. Forms/C.2118/12.

Army Form C. 2118.

Instructions regarding War Diaries and Intelligence Summaries are contained in F. S. Regs., Part II. and the Staff Manual respectively. Title Pages will be prepared in manuscript.

WAR DIARY
or
INTELLIGENCE SUMMARY
(Erase heading not required.)

April 1917

Place	Date	Hour	Summary of Events and Information	Remarks and references to Appendices
ARRAS	1 to 6th		Personnel of Battery employed on building O.Ps for Div. Arty	
SIMENCOURT	7		Battery proceeds to Rest billets at SIMENCOURT. Bty Signallers attached to 48th A.F.A. Bde	
	8		Capt E.W. LOWE RFA attached to 41st Infy. Bde H.Q as Liaison officer. 2Lt J. THOMSON-EVANS assumes Command of Battery	
	9 to 18		Battery in rest Billets at SIMENCOURT	
	15		Battery telephonists returns to Battery.	
ARRAS	18		Capt E.W. LOWE RFA returns & takes over Command of Battery. Battery returns to billets at ARRAS.	
	18 to 30		~~Battery~~ Personnel of Battery employed daily on work for 14th Div. Arty.	
	30		Capt. E.W. LOWE R.F.A. attaches 41st Inf Bde H.Q. as Liaison Officer. 2Lt J. THOMSON-EVANS assumes Command of Battery	

2449 Wt. W14957/M90 750,000 1/16 J.B.C. & A. Forms/C.2118/12.

[illegible] 2Lt. RFA
Commanding V/14 H.T.M. B5

Vol 14

C O N F I D E N T I A L.

W A R D I A R Y,

O F .

X, Y, Z and V/14 DIVISIONAL TRENCH MORTAR BTYS.

From 1st May, 1917 to 31st May, 1917.

Instructions regarding War Diaries and Intelligence Summaries are contained in F. S. Regs., Part II. and the Staff Manual respectively. Title Pages will be prepared in manuscript.

WAR DIARY for 2/14 T M Bty
~~INTELLIGENCE SUMMARY~~
(Erase heading not required.)

Army Form C. 2118.

Place	Date	Hour	Summary of Events and Information	Remarks and references to Appendices
Arras	1 May to 3 May		Bty attchd 46 Bde RFA Working party.	
	4		Working Party attched Ammunition Reserve Park.	
	5		Signallers rejoined from liaison work with Arty. Inspection by DTMO	
	6		Bty left Arras for billets in Achicourt	
Achicourt	7-8		Drill etc.	
	9		Bty to 3rd Army School of Mortars. made up to full strength viz 2 Officers 23 OR by 9 OR's from 1/14 T M Bty.	
	10-19		Redrilling at 3rd Army School of Mortars. Returned from School 19th.	
	20		Rifle Practice.	
	21		Digging T.M. Emplacement for one gun to fire on Sap	
	22		Gun taking up to line. One officer, Lieut Douglass, 1 Servant & 4 OR's up the line with gun	
	23-31		One gun in action in front of CHERISY. Rounds fired NIL. Remainder of Bty Physical Drill etc	

[signature] Lt R.E.
2/14 T M Bty.

2449 Wt. W14957/M90 750,000 1/16 J.B.C. & A. Forms/C.2118/12.

Instructions regarding War Diaries and Intelligence Summaries are contained in F. S. Regs., Part II. and the Staff Manual respectively. Title Pages will be prepared in manuscript.

WAR DIARY or ~~INTELLIGENCE~~ SUMMARY for MAY 1917. of Y. 14. T M. Battery.

(Erase heading not required.)

Army Form C. 2118.

Place	Date	Hour	Summary of Events and Information	Remarks and references to Appendices
	May. 1.		Whole Battery with 47 Brigade - making Gun Positions near WANCOURT.	
	2.		Still Employed with 47 Brigade.	
	3.		Men returned.	
	4.		5 men help to make up a party of 14 men + 1 N.C.O. at work at A.R.P. (M. 14 central).	
	5.		Training at ARRAS. Inspection by D.T.M.O. in morning. Party of 5 men + 1 N.C.O. at work with 46 Brigade	
	6.		Church parade.	
	7.		Moved to ACHICOURT. - into well Barn.	
	8.		Shifted into Gun-positions in Quarry. 2 men at R.A. - Carpentry.	
	9.		Training: Physical Drill, Rifle + Revolver Exercises. Two men returned from R.A.	
	10		"	
	11		Town Major's Party of 20 men made up from "Y" + "Z".	
	12.		Preparation of Range for Rifle + Revolver firing in Quarry.	
	13.		Each man fired 10 rds. (Rifle) at 50 yds:- preceded by "Δ of error" etc.	
	14-16.		Training as above.	
	17.		2 men to C.R.A., + 7 men for Town Major.	
	18.		Training. D.T.M.O. with 2/Lt. Edwards + Sgt. Walmsley reconnoitred front line - Robin Trench	
	19.		2/Lt. Edwards with 12 men proceed to dig Gun-position. One driver wounded by shellfire near WANCOURT.	
	20.		8 men to A.R.P.	
	21-24.		Training as above - Each man fires 10 rds. Rifle + 6 Revolver.	
	25.		4 men at R.A.H.Q. Bdr. Daniel proceeds on Leave.	
	26.		2 " - - Remainder of men fired 6 rds Revolver - Bomb Throwing Practice	
	27.		2 - - Rifle firing by remainder.	
	28-30.		Training as above.	
	31.		7 men with R.A. Signals.	

S. M. Edwards 2/Lt. 6. D.W.

for OC Y. 14. T.M.B.

2449 Wt. W14957/M90 750,000 1/16 J.B.C. & A. Forms/C.2118/12.

Instructions regarding War Diaries and Intelligence Summaries are contained in F. S. Regs., Part II. and the Staff Manual respectively. Title Pages will be prepared in manuscript.

WAR DIARY of Z/14 T.M. Bty. ~~INTELLIGENCE SUMMARY~~

(Erase heading not required.)

Army Form C. 2118.

Place	Date	Hour	Summary of Events and Information	Remarks and references to Appendices
Arras.	1/5/17		2/Lt P. J. Lamb R.G.A joined Bty. Working on gun position for Div. Arty.	
	2		do	
	3		Working party returned early in morning	
	4		4 men and N.C.O to Ammunition Reserve Park.	
	5 & 6		Parades. Inspection by D.T.M.O	
~~Agny~~ Achicourt	7		Bty proceeded to ~~Agny~~ Achicourt	
	8, 9, 10		Parades and fatigues 2/Lt P. J. Lamb R.G.A admitted to Hospital Sick.	
	11		Working party of 1 N.C.O and 12 men for Town Major Achicourt. 3 Gnrs & 6 Ptes (attached) proceeded to 3rd Army School of Mortars with X/14 T.M. Bty for redrilling	
	12		Inspection by C.O. Physical drill and fatigues. Building a rifle range	
	13		Rifle shooting for all ranks. Signaller attached to 43rd Infty Bde.	
	14		Inspection by C.O Physical Drill and marching drill. One officer Lt G. W. Jones & servant attached to 41 Infty Bde for Liaison Work 2/Lt E.W. Edwards commanding Bty in his absence.	
	15 & 16		Physical drill etc.	
	17		Lt G. W. Jones and servant returned from 41st Infty Bde 2/Lt P. J. Lamb rejoined Bty.	
	18		1 N.C.O & 4 men proceeded to BEAURAINS as guard to a dump.	
	19.		Lt G. W. Jones and Servant 18 O.R's of Bty and 5 X/14 T.M. Bty proceeded to 3rd Army School of Mortars for redrilling. Started building T.M. Emplacement in view of placing 2" T.M in line again.	
	20 to 28		Physical Training. Rifle Shooting etc.	

2449 Wt. W14957/M90 750,000 1/16 J.B.C. & A. Forms/C.2118/12.

Army Form C. 2118.

Instructions regarding War Diaries and Intelligence Summaries are contained in F. S. Regs., Part II. and the Staff Manual respectively. Title Pages will be prepared in manuscript.

WAR DIARY or INTELLIGENCE SUMMARY

of 2/1st T. M Bty (cont)

(Erase heading not required.)

Place	Date	Hour	Summary of Events and Information	Remarks and references to Appendices
~~Army~~ Acheux	29		Bty returned from 3rd Army School of Mortars.	
	30		Inspection by C.O. Physical Drill etc	
	31.		do "	

G. D. Jones. Lieut R.G.A.
O.C. 2/1st T. M Bty.

2449 Wt. W14957/M90 750,000 1/16 J.B.C. & A. Forms/C.2118/12.

Army Form C. 2118.

Instructions regarding War Diaries and Intelligence Summaries are contained in F. S. Regs., Part II. and the Staff Manual respectively. Title Pages will be prepared in manuscript.

V/14 HEAVY TRENCH MORTAR BATTERY.
Date 31.5.17

WAR DIARY
or
INTELLIGENCE SUMMARY
(Erase heading not required.)

May 1917

Place	Date	Hour	Summary of Events and Information	Remarks and references to Appendices
ARRAS	1 2		Personnel of Battery employed on work for 14th DIV. ARTY.	
	3		Capt. E. W. LOWE R.F.A returns & takes over Command of Battery after acting as Liaison Officer with 41st Infy Bde H.Q.	
Sheet 51B	7		Battery vacates billets at ARRAS and proceeds to billets at ACHICOURT	
32.c.6.4	8 to 22		35 men attached to Kings Liverpool Regt. for road making	
	9		Signallers attached to 41st I.Bde on Liaison duty.	
	14		2 9.45" trench mortars handed over to V/37 H.T.M.Bty	
	23		Capt. E. W. LOWE RFA relinquishes Command of Battery on being posted to A/46 Bde R.F.A.	
	24		2Lt. J. THOMSON-EVANS R.F.A assumes Command of Batty with rank of Acting Captain.	
			2 9.45" trench mortars handed over to VI Corps.	
			Working parties employed daily for duty with 14th Div. F.A. Bdes.	
	29		Gnrs ROBINSON and BOUQUET awarded Military Medals for acts of gallantry in the Field during recent operations.	

J Thomson Evans. Capt. R.F.A.
Comdg V/14 Hvy T. M. Batty.

2449 Wt. W14957/M90 750,000 1/16 J.B.C. & A. Forms/C.2118/12.

Army Form C. 2118.

Instructions regarding War Diaries and Intelligence Summaries are contained in F. S. Regs., Part II. and the Staff Manual respectively. Title Pages will be prepared in manuscript.

WAR DIARY
or ~~INTELLIGENCE SUMMARY~~ 2/14 T.M. Bty.

(*Erase heading not required.*)

Place	Date	Hour	Summary of Events and Information	Remarks and references to Appendices
Agny.	1st June to 27th June.		Training:- Physical Drill, Rifle & Revolver shooting, signalling marching etc.	
Etree-wamin	28th		Left Agny for Etree-wamin billeted for night	
Croix	29th		Left Etree-wamin for Croix	
"	30		Resting at Croix	

[illegible] 2/Lt for Lieut RFA
O.C. 2/14 T.M. Bty.

2449 Wt. W14957/M90 750,000 1/16 J.B.C. & A. Forms/C.2118/12.

Army Form C. 2118.

Instructions regarding War Diaries and Intelligence Summaries are contained in F. S. Regs., Part II. and the Staff Manual respectively. Title Pages will be prepared in manuscript.

WAR DIARY
or
~~INTELLIGENCE~~ SUMMARY
(Erase heading not required.)

of Y. 14. T. M. Battery.
for. June. 1917.

Place	Date	Hour	Summary of Events and Information	Remarks and references to Appendices
ACHICOURT.	1st – 14th		Seven men at work at Divisional A.R.P.	
			Remainder of Battery Training:- Physical Drill, Signalling, Bombing, Shooting (Rifle & Revolver) Artillery foot Drill, Respirator Drill etc.	
LIGNY – St FLOCHEL.	15th to 30th		Whole of Battery at 3rd Army T. M. School Re-drilling.	
–	30th		Battery returned to Division.	

J. R. Cranmer Lt R.F.A.
O.C. Y. 14. T.M.B.

2449 Wt. W14957/M90 750,000 1/16 J.B.C. & A. Forms/C.2118/12.

Army Form C. 2118.

Instructions regarding War Diaries and Intelligence Summaries are contained in F. S. Regs., Part II. and the Staff Manual respectively. Title Pages will be prepared in manuscript.

WAR DIARY or ~~INTELLIGENCE SUMMARY~~ 2/1st T. M. Bty.

(Erase heading not required.)

Place	Date	Hour	Summary of Events and Information	Remarks and references to Appendices
Field	June 1st to 27th		Training Physical Drill, Rifle & Revolver shooting, marching drill, Signalling etc.	
	15th		1 O R to School of Mortars 3rd Army with Y/1st T M Bty.	
	23rd		Smoke Helmet Inspection.	
	26.		Gymnastic Competition with V/1st Heavy T M Bty.	
	28th		Bty started on march at 9 am for an unknown destination arrived at Etree-wamin in evening	
	29th		marched from Etree-wamin to Croix and billeted for night	
	30th		Stayed at Croix for day starting march tomorrow (1st May)	

G. S. Jones. Lieut R.F.A.
2/1st T. M. Bty

13

Instructions regarding War Diaries and Intelligence Summaries are contained in F. S. Regs., Part II. and the Staff Manual respectively. Title Pages will be prepared in manuscript.

WAR DIARY
or
~~INTELLIGENCE SUMMARY~~
(Erase heading not required.)

14 D T M Bty
June 1917.
Vol 15

Army Form C. 2118.

Place	Date	Hour	Summary of Events and Information	Remarks and references to Appendices
Sheet 51B 32.c.6.4	1 to 27		Battery at rest in billets at ACHICOURT	
	19		Capt J. THOMSON-EVANS proceeds on leave to England. 2Lt E.F. MELLOR assumes command of Battery.	
	28		Battery vacates Billets at ACHICOURT and proceeds to billets at ETRE-WAMIN	
	29		Battery proceeds to Billets at EROIX	
	30		Battery at rest in Billets at ~~[illegible]~~ EAM. CROIX	

E.F. Mellor 2/Lt. R.F.A.
Comdg V/14 H.T.M. Bty.

2449 Wt. W14957/M90 750,000 1/16 J.B.C. & A. Forms/C.2118/12.

C O N F I D E N T I A L.

W A R   D I A R Y.

O F.

TRENCH MORTAR BATTERIES, 14TH DIVISION.

From July 1st, 1917 to - July 31st, 1917.

VOLUME 27.

Instructions regarding War Diaries and Intelligence Summaries are contained in F. S. Regs., Part II. and the Staff Manual respectively. Title Pages will be prepared in manuscript.

WAR DIARY ~~or~~ ~~INTELLIGENCE SUMMARY~~ of X/14 T M Bty

(Erase heading not required.)

Army Form C. 2118.

July 1917.

Place	Date	Hour	Summary of Events and Information	Remarks and references to Appendices
	1st		Bty vacated billets a CROIX & proceeded to billets at NEDONCHELLE	
	2		Bty proceeded to billets at Aire	
	3		" " " Strazeele	
	4		" " " St Jans Capel	
	5		" in rest in billets at "	
	6		" proceeded to billets at Dränoutre	
	7 to 10		" in rest at billets at "	
	11		Working Party to 46 Bde R.F.A. 5 O.R's. remainder of battery proceeded to billets at St Jans Capel. Lieut A. M Douglas O.C. Bty proceeded on leave to England.	
	12		Bty in rest at billets in St Jans Capel	
	13		Working Party to 47 Bde R.F.A. 4 O.R's.	
	14-17		Bty still in rest. 2/Lt W. Pope proceeded on leave to England (17)	
	18-26		" " " 1 O R wounded in action. Lieut A. M Douglas rejoined from leave (25)	
	27		Working party to 46 Bde R.F.A. 4 O R's.	
	28		2/Lt W Pope rejoined from leave.	
	29-30		Remainder of Bty at rest. Left for billets at CROIX DE POPERINGHE	
	31		Bty at rest.	

A M Douglas
Lieut R.F.A
O.C. X/14 T M Bty.

2449 Wt. W14957/M90 750,000 1/16 J.B.C. & A. Forms/C.2118/12.

Army Form C. 2118.

Instructions regarding War Diaries and Intelligence Summaries are contained in F. S. Regs., Part II. and the Staff Manual respectively. Title Pages will be prepared in manuscript.

WAR DIARY or ~~INTELLIGENCE SUMMARY~~ of Y. 14 T.M. Battery for July 1917.

(Erase heading not required.)

Place	Date	Hour	Summary of Events and Information	Remarks and references to Appendices
CROIX.	1st		Battery left CROIX for HERNE. Gr. Devan. J. went on Leave.	
HERNE.	2.		Marched from Herne to St Martin.	
St MARTIN	3.		Travelled by Lorry from St Martin to Strazeele.	
STRAZEELE	4.		From Strazeele to Bailleul by Lorry.	
BAILLEUL.	5.		Training at Bailleul.	
"	6.		Marched from Bailleul to Dranoutre.	
DRANOUTRE	7.		Battery Training.	
"	8.		Church Parade.	
"	9-10.		Training.	
"	11.		Returned to Bailleul. 4 men at work for 46 Brigade	
BAILLEUL	12.		Drill.	
"	13.		1 N.C.O. + 9 men at work for 47 Brigade.	
"	14.		Training.	
"	15.		" Gr. Stratford went on Leave.	
"	16-20.		"	
"	21.		1 N.C.O. + 9 men returned from 47 Brigade.	
"	22-27.		Battery Training. Gr. Gaffney. J. went on Leave. (27)	
"	28-29		Training. Gr. Nolan on Leave. (29)	
"	30.		Left Bailleul for Croix de Poperinghe.	
CROIX. de. POPERINGHE	31.		Drill + Baths at St Jans Cappel.	

[illegible] Lt. 6th C.I.
for O.C. Y. 14. T.M.B.

2449 Wt. W14957/M90 750,000 1/16 J.B.C. & A. Forms/C.2118/12.

Instructions regarding War Diaries and Intelligence Summaries are contained in F. S. Regs., Part II. and the Staff Manual respectively. Title Pages will be prepared in manuscript.

Army Form C. 2118.

WAR DIARY
or
~~INTELLIGENCE~~ SUMMARY

Z/14 T.M. Batty. (Erase heading not required.) July 1917.

Place	Date	Hour	Summary of Events and Information	Remarks and references to Appendices
	1		March continued. Moved from Croix to NEDAUCHEL	
	2		Moved from NEDAUCHEL to ST MARTIN	
	3		" " ST MARTIN to STRAZEELE.	
	4		Stayed at STRAZEELE	
	5		Moved to ST JANS CAPEL	
	6		Stayed at " "	
	7		Moved to DRANOUTRE.	
	8 to 10		Stayed at DRANOUTRE	
ST JANS CAPEL	11		Moved back to ST JANS CAPEL and went under Canvas. 1 N.C.O. and 4 men attached to 46th Bde R.F.A. for work.	
	12		Training & redrilling restarted.	
	13		1 N.C.O. and 12 men attached to 47th Bde RFA for work	
	14 to 19		Remainder of Batty continue training.	
	20		11 Infantrymen attached to Battery returned to their respective Units.	
	21		1 N.C.O and 8 men returned to Battery from 47th Bde RFA.	
	22 to 24		Training Continued.	
	25		Lt. G.W. JONES R.FA proceeded on leave to U.K	
	26 to 29		Training Continued	
Sheet 28 M.32.d.9.7	30		Battery proceeds to Billets at 28.M.32.d.9.7.	

J. S. Ogilvie 2 Lt RFA
Comdg Z/14 T.M. Batty.

2449 Wt. W14957/M90 750,000 1/16 J.B.C. & A. Forms/C.2118/12.

Army Form C. 2118.

WAR DIARY
or
~~INTELLIGENCE SUMMARY~~
(Erase heading not required.)

Instructions regarding War Diaries and Intelligence Summaries are contained in F. S. Regs., Part II and the Staff Manual respectively. Title Pages will be prepared in manuscript.

V/14 HEAVY TRENCH MORTAR BATTERY. No. 13/1

July 1917.

Place	Date	Hour	Summary of Events and Information	Remarks and references to Appendices
	1		Battery vacated billets at CROIX + proceeded to billets at NEDAUCHEL.	
	2		Battery proceeded to billets at AIRE	
	3	"	" " " " " STRAZEELE	
	4		" " " " " ST. JANS CAPEL	
	5		Battery in rest at Billets at " " "	
	6		Battery proceeded to Billets at DRANOUTRE	
	7 to 10		Battery in rest at Billets at "	
	10		Working party of 13 men attached to C/46 Bde R.F.A. for digging gun positions.	
	11		Battery proceeded to Billets at ST JANS CAPEL	
	12 [illegible]		Battery in rest at Billets at ST JANS CAPEL	
	13		Remaining available personnel employed on working parties with 47th Bde RFA.	
	16		Party of 13 men return from C/46 Bde R.F.A.	

2449 Wt. W14957/M90 750,000 1/16 J.B.C. & A. Forms/C.2118/12.

*Instructions regarding War Diaries and Intelligence Summaries are contained in F. S. Regs., Part II and the Staff Manual respectively. Title Pages will be prepared in manuscript.

V/14
HEAVY TRENCH
MORTAR BATTERY.
13/2

WAR DIARY
or
INTELLIGENCE SUMMARY
(Erase heading not required.)

Army Form C. 2118.

Place	Date	Hour	Summary of Events and Information	Remarks and references to Appendices
1	17		Working party at 47th Bde suffer 5 Casualties.	
	20		Working parties return from 47th Bde RFA.	
	24	"	Working party attached to C/46 Bde RFA	
	25 to 29		Remainder of Battery in rest at Billets at ST JANS CAPEL	
	30		Batty proceeded to Billets at 28. M. 32. d. 9. 7.	

Thomson Evans.
Capt. R.F.A.
Comdg V/14 Hvy T. M. Bty

2449 Wt. W14957/M90 750,000 1/16 J.B.C. & A. Forms/C.2118/12.

Vol 17

War Diary for

Medium and Heavy Trench Mortar Batteries 14 Division

—

August – 1917.

Army Form C. 2118.

Instructions regarding War Diaries and Intelligence Summaries are contained in F. S. Regs., Part II. and the Staff Manual respectively. Title Pages will be prepared in manuscript.

WAR DIARY X/47 T.M. Bty
or
INTELLIGENCE SUMMARY
(*Erase heading not required.*)

August 1917.

Place	Date	Hour	Summary of Events and Information	Remarks and references to Appendices
	1st		1 Officer & 4 O.R.'s to School of Mortars Second Army on course of 6" newton T.M.	
	2		1 O.R. from D/46 Bde R.F.A. 1 O.R. wounded in action	
	3		Training	
	4		3 O.R.'s from D/47 Bde R.F.A. (Isolated owing to coming in contact with case of scarlet fever)	
	5-7		Training	
	8		1 O.R. to Hospital	
	9-10		Training	
	11		Left Croix de Poperinghe for billets at Reninghelst	
	12-20		Training	
	21		1 Officer & 4 O.R.'s from School of Mortars, Second Army.	
	22-29		Training	
	30		1 Officer reconnoitred position for 6" newton T.M.	
	31		Position being built for 6" newton T.M. Two O.R.'s to 46 Bde R.F.A. for duty.	

[illegible] Lieut R.F.A.
O.C. X/47 T.M. Bty.

Army Form C. 2118.

Instructions regarding War Diaries and Intelligence Summaries are contained in F. S. Regs., Part II. and the Staff Manual respectively. Title Pages will be prepared in manuscript.

WAR DIARY
or
~~INTELLIGENCE SUMMARY~~ for. August 1917.
(Erase heading not required.)

Y/14 MEDIUM TRENCH MORTAR BATTERY. Date 31. 8. 17.

Place	Date	Hour	Summary of Events and Information	Remarks and references to Appendices
CROIX de. POPERINGHE.	Aug: 1.		In Camp at CROIX de POPERINGHE.	
"	2.		Gr DERVAN. wounded while at work on Battery Position with 47th Bde.	
			Gr WOODS went on Leave.	
"	4.		Gr STAFF. went on Leave. N.C.O. & 4 men returned from 47 Bde. These men were isolated 14 days, as case of Scarlet Fever had occurred while in Trenches.	
"	11.		Moved by Lorry to RENINGHELST.	
RENINGHELST.	15.		Baths.	
"	16.		Route March.	
"	18.		Baths & change of Underclothing.	
"	19.		Church Parade in Y.M.C.A Hut.	
"	20.		Gr SHAW. - Orderly at D.A.	
"	23.		1 Cpl & 6 men at work on Track with 89th F. Coy:	
"	26.		Party returned from 89th F. Coy:	
"	29.		Route March.	
"	31.		1 Cpl. & 1 man with Lt Jones on 6" Emplacement near STIRLING CASTLE.	
			2 men at Wagon Lines.	

E. W. Edwards. 2Lt.
Y. 14. T.M. B.

2449 Wt. W14957/M90 750,000 1/16 J.B.C. & A. Forms/C.2118/12.

Instructions regarding War Diaries and Intelligence Summaries are contained in F. S. Regs., Part II. and the Staff Manual respectively. Title Pages will be prepared in manuscript.

WAR DIARY or INTELLIGENCE SUMMARY

(Erase heading not required.)

Z/14 T M Bty

Army Form C. 2118.

August 1917.

Place	Date	Hour	Summary of Events and Information	Remarks and references to Appendices
Field	1		One Gnr to England (under age). 4 O R's to School of Mortars Second Army for course on 6" newton T.M.	
	2		Two O R's rejoined from Working Party 46 Bde R.F.A.	
	3-5		Training. 3 O Rs rejoined from Working Party 47 Bde R.F.A. (5)	
	6		C.C. rejoined from leave of absence to England.	
	7-10		Training	
	11		Left Croix de Poperinghe for billets at Reninghelst	
	12-18		Training. 1 O R attached 14 D A C for duty (13)	
	19		Church Parade. Inspection by C.C.	
	20		Training	
	21		4 O R's from School of Mortars Second Army.	
	22		Training	
	23		4 O R's attached 89 Field Coy R.E. for duty.	
	24		1 O R to 14 D A for duty.	
	25		Sergt to Hospital (Sick)	
	26-29		Training	
	30		Reconnoitred suitable position for 6" Newton T.M.	

2449 Wt. W14957/M90 750,000 1/16 J.B.C. & A. Forms/C.2118/12.

Army Form C. 2118.

Instructions regarding War Diaries and Intelligence Summaries are contained in F. S. Regs., Part II. and the Staff Manual respectively. Title Pages will be prepared in manuscript.

WAR DIARY or INTELLIGENCE SUMMARY

of X/51 T M Bty (cont)

(Erase heading not required.)

Place	Date	Hour	Summary of Events and Information	Remarks and references to Appendices
	31		Position for 6" Newton T. M. being built. 2 OR's attached to 46 Bde R.FA for duty.	
			G. S. Jones Lieut RFA. O.C. X/51 T M Bty.	

2449 Wt. W14957/M90 750,000 1/16 J.B.C. & A. Forms/C.2118/12.

Instructions regarding War Diaries and Intelligence Summaries are contained in F. S. Regs., Part II. and the Staff Manual respectively. Title Pages will be prepared in manuscript.

WAR DIARY
or
~~INTELLIGENCE SUMMARY~~
(Erase heading not required.)

August.

V/14 HEAVY TRENCH MORTAR BATTERY.
No. 14/1
Date.

Army Form C. 2118.

Place	Date	Hour	Summary of Events and Information	Remarks and references to Appendices
CROIX DE POPERINGHE	1		1 Officer and 11 O.R. proceed to 2nd Army School of Mortars on a 3 weeks course. Capt J. Thomson-Evans proceeding ~~to~~ as the officer.	
			2/Lt E. F. Mellor takes over command of Battery in billets at CROIX DE POPERINGHE	
	2 } 10 }		Battery in Billets at CROIX DE POPERINGHE.	
RENINGHELST	11		Battery vacates Billets at " " " and proceeds to RENINGHELST.	
	13		2/Lt J. P. F. Ogilvie proceeds to England on leave.	
	21		Capt J. Thomson Evans returns from Course at 2nd Army School of mortars & takes over command of Battery. 11 O.R. return to Battery after course.	
	22		~~[illegible]~~ ~~4~~ 5 9.45" Trench mortars taken over from 18th Div. Trench Mortars, in the line. (not in action).	
	23.		Working party of 20 O.Ranks attached to 89th Field Coy R.E. for duty.	
	24		6 ~~4~~ 9.45" Trench Mortars taken over from 56th Div. Trench mortars.	
	26		Working party returns from 89th Fd. Coy R.E. 2/Lt J.P.F. Ogilvie returns from leave. 1 N.C.O. and 4 men attached as runners to "A" Group Field Artillery.	

2449 Wt. W14957/M90 750,000 1/16 J.B.C. & A. Forms/C.2118/12.

Instructions regarding War Diaries and Intelligence Summaries are contained in F. S. Regs., Part II. and the Staff Manual respectively. Title Pages will be prepared in manuscript.

WAR DIARY
or
INTELLIGENCE SUMMARY
(Erase heading not required.)

V/14 HEAVY TRENCH MORTAR BATTERY. No. 14/2 Date.

Army Form C. 2118.

Place	Date	Hour	Summary of Events and Information	Remarks and references to Appendices
RENINGHELST	31		Working party of 20 Other Ranks attached to 46th Bde RFA for duty.	

J Mansan-Evans. Capt RFA.
Comdg V/14 H.T. M. Batty.

2449 Wt. W14957/M90 750,000 1/16 J.B.C. & A. Forms/C.2118/12.

Vol 18

W A R   D I A R Y

TRENCH MORTAR BATTERIES 14TH DIVISION

(X/14, Y/14, Z/14 and V/14 H.T.M.)

FOR

S E P T E M B E R   1 9 1 7.

==*=*=*=*=*

11

Instructions regarding War Diaries and Intelligence Summaries are contained in F. S. Regs., Part II. and the Staff Manual respectively. Title Pages will be prepared in manuscript.

X/14 MEDIUM TRENCH MORTAR BATTERY. No. Sept 17 Date

Army Form C. 2118.

WAR DIARY for SEPTEMBER 1917 ~~INTELLIGENCE~~ SUMMARY

(Erase heading not required.)

X/14 T.M. BTY.

Place	Date	Hour	Summary of Events and Information	Remarks and references to Appendices
RENINGHELST	1.	—	Battery in camp at Reninghelst. Gr. Wright proceeds on leave	
	2.	—	2 aeroplane bombs dropped in camp, 1 man (Gr Cook Y/14) killed 1 (Gr Rankin V/14) wounded.	
	3.	—	all batteries attend funeral of Gr Cook. Capt LESTER officiating	
	4	—	~~Gr. Tippetts to hospital~~	
	6	—	Leave camp for BAILLEUL by lorry	
BAILLEUL	7	—	Park guns & stores in new camp (France Sheet 28 - S 22 a 4.2)	
	8.	—	Working party for 40th Bde. R.F.A. X/14 supplying 4 men.	
	10	—	Grs ASHLEY, COLLINS O'CALLAGHAN posted to the Bty from 14 D.A.C.	
	12.	—	1 n.c.o. & 2 men at work on ammunition dump.	
	17.	—	Bdr. Johnston proceeds on leave.	
	23.	—	Gr. Butler " " "	
		—	Sergt Woodward & 8 men form working party of 50 at 89 Field Coy R.E.s	

A. W. Douglas Lieut R.F.A. O.C. X/14 T.M. Bty.

2449 Wt. W14957/M90 750,000 1/16 J.B.C. & A. Forms/C.2118/12.

Instructions regarding War Diaries and Intelligence Summaries are contained in F. S. Regs., Part II. and the Staff Manual respectively. Title Pages will be prepared in manuscript.

WAR DIARY
or
~~INTELLIGENCE SUMMARY~~
(Erase heading not required.)

Army Form C. 2118.

for SEPTEMBER.
Y. 14 TRENCH MORTAR BATTERY.

Place	Date	Hour	Summary of Events and Information	Remarks and references to Appendices
RENINGHELST.	Sept. 1.		Battery in Camp at Reninghelst.	
	- 2.		Cpl Illingworth & 3 men fetch Newton 3rd (6"). Remainder of Battery building sandbag walls around Huts.	
			Gr Cook killed by Aeroplane Bomb, 10.45 pm.	
	3.		Gr Cook buried in Reninghelst Cemetery by Capt. Lester. All batteries attended funeral.	
	4 to 5.		Continued building Sandbag shelters.	
	5.		Moved by Lorry to Bailleul.	
BAILLEUL.	7.		Parked Guns & Stores.	
	8.9 & 10.		14 men with 4 N.C.O.s left Camp at 6.30 am. for work with 46. Bde.	
	11.		Gr Diamond & Gr Martin joined Battery from D.A.C. Gr Rice goes on Leave.	
	12.		" " " " " at work on Amn Dump.	
	13.		Gr Hallam & Gr Gaffney sent to Hospital from 46 Bde.	
	14-15. 16.		2 NCO's & 4 men returned from 46 Bde.	
	20.		Baths & change of Underclothing.	
	21.		Sgt. Walmsley on Leave. Gr Elkin relieved Gr Shaw at C.R.A.	
	22.		2 N.C.O's & 6 men returned from 46 Bde.	
	23.		Gr Shaw goes on Leave.	
			Bdr Atkinson & 5 men returned to 46 Bde.	
	23-30.			

L.M. Edwards. Lt.
O.C. Y. 14 T.M.B.

2449 Wt. W14957/M90 750,000 1/16 J.B.C. & A. Forms/C.2118/12.

Army Form C. 2118.

Instructions regarding War Diaries and Intelligence Summaries are contained in F. S. Regs., Part II. and the Staff Manual respectively. Title Pages will be prepared in manuscript.

WAR DIARY
or
~~INTELLIGENCE SUMMARY~~

of Z/14 T M Bty

(Erase heading not required.)

September 1917

Place	Date	Hour	Summary of Events and Information	Remarks and references to Appendices
Field	1st to 3rd		Training. 6" Newton Bty taken out of position in line 1st.	
	4th		Two O.R's returned from 46th Bde R.F.A. and one O.R from 1st D.A.C.	
	5		Training	
	6		Bty moved from Reninghelst to billets at 28 S 22 a 4.2.	
	7		One O.R on leave. One O.R admitted Hospital at Base.	
	8		13 O.R's attached to 47 Bde R.F.A for duty.	
	9		1 do posted Bty from D.A.C as reinforcement	
			1 do rejoined from attached 1st D.A.C.	
	10		Reconnoitred in line for 6" Newton T.M. position.	
	11		One O.R attached to Corps Ammunition Railhead Officer for duty	
	12-15		Training	
	16		12 O.R's rejoined from 46 Bde R.F.A.	
	17-22		Training. Two 6" Newton T.M's drawn from D.A.D.O.S. [illegible]	
	23		~~Training~~ 2 O.R's attached 89 Field Coy R.E. for duty.	
	25		1 N.C.O leave to England.	
	26-30		Training	

G. S. Jones
Lieut R.F.A.
OC Z/14 T.M. Bty.

2449 Wt. W14957/M90 750,000 1/16 J.B.C. & A. Forms/C.2118/12.

Instructions regarding War Diaries and Intelligence Summaries are contained in F. S. Regs., Part II. and the Staff Manual respectively. Title Pages will be prepared in manuscript.

WAR DIARY
or
INTELLIGENCE SUMMARY
(Erase heading not required.)

Army Form C. 2118.

V/14 HEAVY TRENCH MORTAR BATTERY.
No. ....
Date. ....

September.

Place	Date	Hour	Summary of Events and Information	Remarks and references to Appendices
RENINGHELST	1		Battery in Billets at RENINGHELST	"
	3		Gnr. LARKIN wounded by enemy bomb.	
B22.a.2.0	6		Battery proceeds to Billets at LEE FARM. S.22.a.2.0	
	8		32 men attached to F.A. Bdes on working parties.	
	10		10 reinforcements received from 14th D.A.C.	
	11		1 sergeant and 10 men attached to C.A.R.O at KENNEBAK railhead for duty	
	20		32 men attached F.A. Bdes on working parties return to Battery.	
	23		1 officer and 30 other ranks attached to 89th Fd. Coy. RE's	

J. Rawson-Evans. Capt RFA
Comdg V/14 HTM Bty

2449 Wt. W14957/M90 750,000 1/16 J.B.C. & A. Forms/C.2118/12.

W A R D I A R Y O F

X/14 , Y /14, Z/14, and V/14 T.M.BATTERIES

14TH DIVISION.

O C T O B E R - 1 9 1 7

=======

Vol 19

Army Form C. 2118.

Instructions regarding War Diaries and Intelligence Summaries are contained in F. S. Regs., Part II. and the Staff Manual respectively. Title Pages will be prepared in manuscript.

WAR DIARY or ~~INTELLIGENCE SUMMARY~~

X/1st T M Bty.

(Erase heading not required.)

October 1917

Place	Date	Hour	Summary of Events and Information	Remarks and references to Appendices
	3-10		Training	
	5		Bty left Lee Farm (28 S 22 a 1.1) for 28 I 5 d 8.4)	
	5½?		Lieut A.M. Douglass proceeds on 6 months leave to Australia. struck off strength. 1 N C O and 2 O R's to return from Amm. Dump.	
	15?		2/Lt W. Pope posted to R.F.C. from this date leaves bty to proceed to R.F.C. H.Q. 2/Lt Northfield joins Bty. proceed up to the line with working party to work on new position on left of divisional front.	
	16-20		Work proceeding on left position	
	20		Lt J.W. Hornby joined 1st Div T.M's and proceed up line with D.T.M.O. to view new position on left.	
	21.		O.C.'s X & Z/1st T.M. Batteries and 2/Lt Northfield reconnoitred positions on right of divisional front	
	22 & 23		Work on positions continued. Gun drill on 6" Newton T.M for remaining O.R's.	
	24		Working parties with other units cancelled. Men rejoin bty.	
	25		Permission received from Corps to start work on right position U 11 a 8.5.	
	26		Lts Scott & Hornby to work on new positions. Weather prevented work.	
	27		2/Lt Northfield up line all day on new position U11 a 8.5.	
	28		Work continued	
	29.		Lts Hornby & Northfield proceeded up line to new position. Work progressing well all day.	
	30		X/1st T M Bty fired 24 rounds with new 6" T.M which shot remarkably well.	
	31.		2/Lt Northfield up line to new position all day. 1 O R on leave.	

A J W Hornby
Lieut R.F.A.
O.C. X/1st T.M. Bty.

2449 Wt. W14957/M90 750,000 1/16 J.B.C. & A. Forms/C.2118/12.

Army Form C. 2118.

Instructions regarding War Diaries and Intelligence Summaries are contained in F. S. Regs., Part II. and the Staff Manual respectively. Title Pages will be prepared in manuscript.

WAR DIARY
or
INTELLIGENCE SUMMARY
(*Erase heading not required.*)

Y. 14 TRENCH MORTAR BATTERY, for October 1917.

Place	Date	Hour	Summary of Events and Information	Remarks and references to Appendices
BAILLEUL.	Oct 1.	–	6 men sent to move Amn at T.1.c.3.1.	
			Remainder of Battery with 46 Bde.	
"	2-7.	"	Lt. E.M. EDWARDS reconnoitred Right Half Divisional front with view to putting in 6" NEWTON.	
	3.		Visit Bn Commander 9th RB. Gr Martin sent to Hospital with Scabies.	
"	4		Reconnoitre front line with Intelligence Officer (9th RB)	
"	10.		Moved to WULVERGHEM.	
"	11.		Reconnoitred Trenches with 2 Lt. POPE.	
WULVERGHEM	12.		Men taken to dig position in front line.	
.	13		Completed Trench.	
.	15.		2 Lt. CLARKE joined Y. Battery.	
.	16.		D.T.M.O. taken around Front line.	
			Gr TRAMMER wounded slightly by Shell fire.	
.	17.		Party of 10 men with Cpl ILLINGWORTH in Trenches with 2 days rations digging new position.	
.	18.		Reconnoitred for 6" position on left of 8th Div. front. Gr LOW to Hospital.	
	19.		Gr ELKIN on Leave.	
	20.		Men at work on Position.	
	21.		Baths.	
	22.		Started Canteen	
	23.		Gr DIAMOND on Leave.	
	24-29.		Men at work on Positions.	
	30.		Fired 24 Rounds with Artillery Co-operation upon Batum House & KIWI.	
	31.		Party at work in Trenches.	

31/10/17. E.M. Edwards, Lt. O.C. Y. 14. T.M.B.

2449 Wt. W14957/M90 750,000 1/16 J.B.C. & A. Forms/C.2118/12.

Instructions regarding War Diaries and Intelligence Summaries are contained in F. S. Regs., Part II. and the Staff Manual respectively. Title Pages will be prepared in manuscript.

WAR DIARY
of Z/14 T. M. Bty.
INTELLIGENCE SUMMARY
(Erase heading not required.)

Army Form C. 2118.

October 1917.

Place	Date	Hour	Summary of Events and Information	Remarks and references to Appendices
	1–10		Training	
	11		Lieut G. W. Jones to Hospital sick. Bty left Lee Farm (28 S 22 a 1.1.) for 28 T 5 d 8.4.	
	12–13		Training and parties digging positions.	
	14		Lt G. H. Scott joined 14 Div. T.M's from 14 DAC and posted as O.C. Z/14 T.M Bty vice Lt G. W. Jones to England sick	
	15–25		Parties from Bty building positions on left of divisional front for Y/14 T. M Bty when completed. Work on alternate position also in execution	
	26		OC's X & Z/14 T.M Bttys examined proposed position on right bank of River DOUVE on 8th Divisional front and decided on suitable spot to make gun position for combined X & Z Bttys	
	27		Work on above position started by O R's from X & Z Bttys.	
	28		OC. Z/14 reconnoitring for suitable spot to observe firing on 8th Div. front. No place suitable. Observation post found in support line that could be used for preliminary ranging	
	30		OC Z/14 found good observation post on 33 Div. front line on extreme right flank. was found possible to cross from 33 Div front to 8 Div front in daylight small parties only.	
	31		Working party still building position on 8 Div front	

G. H. Scott. Lieut RFA
O.C. Z/14 T M Bty.

2449 Wt. W14957/M90 750,000 1/16 J.B.C. & A. Forms/C.2118/12.

Instructions regarding War Diaries and Intelligence Summaries are contained in F. S. Regs., Part II. and the Staff Manual respectively. Title Pages will be prepared in manuscript.

V/14 HEAVY TRENCH MORTAR BATTERY. No. 16/1. Date.

WAR DIARY
or
INTELLIGENCE SUMMARY
(Erase heading not required.)

Army Form C. 2118.

October 1917.

Place	Date	Hour	Summary of Events and Information	Remarks and references to Appendices
B.22.a.2.0.	1 To 6		1 Officer + 30 O.Ranks attached 62nd Fd. Coy R.E. for work on Corps Line Trench.	
	2		1 Sgt transferred to 2nd Army T.M. School.	
	4th 16 25th		30 O.Ranks working for 46th Bde R.F.A. on O.P.'s	
	9		1 N.C.O. + 9 men attached 47th Bde RFA on O.P. work.	
	12		Battery vacates Billets at Lee Farm B.22.a.2.0 + proceeds to camp at T.10.d.0.4.	
	24		Working party attached 47th Bde RFA return to Unit.	
	26.		Digging + Carrying Commenced for 9.45 H.T.M. position.	
	27		Cpt. J. Thomson-Evans proceeds on leave to England. 2/Lt. E.J. Mellor assumes temporary command of Battery.	
	28 To 31		Digging on 9.45 H.T.M. Position Continued.	

E J Mellor
2/Lieut R.F.A.
Comdg V/14 Hy T.M. Batty.

2449 Wt. W14957/M90 750,000 1/16 J.B.C. & A. Forms/C.2118/12.

C O N F I D E N T I A L .

Vol 20

W A R   D I A R Y

F O R

N O V E M B E R - 1 9 1 7.

TRENCH MORTAR BATTERIES 14TH DIVISION

(X/14, Y/14, Z/14 M.T.M.Btys. & V/14 H.T.M.Bty.)

NOV	1	Went to new position with Capt Hoather to reconnoitre O.P.'s
	2	Work finished on new pos. Difficulties raised by Battalion as to firing
	3	Went to new Pos with [illegible] + found Co S.M. [illegible] had dismantled [illegible]
	4	Work on Camp
	5	Work on Camp
	6	

2449 Wt. W14957/M90 750,000 1/16 J.B.C. & A. Forms/C.2118/12.

Army Form C. 2118.

Instructions regarding War Diaries and Intelligence Summaries are contained in F. S. Regs., Part II. and the Staff Manual respectively. Title Pages will be prepared in manuscript.

WAR DIARY of X/14 T M Bty
~~or INTELLIGENCE SUMMARY~~

(Erase heading not required.)

Novr.

Place	Date	Hour	Summary of Events and Information	Remarks and references to Appendices
	Novr.			
WULVERGHEM	7		Gun Drill, construction of New Dug Outs & General Camp Improvements	
"	8			
"	9			
"	10			
"	11	- - -	Construction of new 6" T.M. Bed (sub) Gun Drill & laying with 6" T.M.	
"	12			
"	13			
"	14		Salving of unexpended ammunition, shell cases &c &c & 1 hours Gun Drill per day	
"	15			
"	16			
"	17			
"	18	- - -	Moved to Watou by Motor Lorry	
"	19	- - -	Overhauling & cleaning guns & stores. 2 hours Morse Signalling with Flags	
"	20	- - -	8 Men proceeded at 5 a.m. to Pickering Dump St Jeanne for attachment for Duty	
"	21		Remainder of Personnel 1 hours drill per day, cleaning of guns & stores & General Camp Fatigues	
"	22			
"	23			
"	24	- - -	Moved to No 15 Camp BRANDHOEK	
"	25		Drill & Camp Fatigues 26th 1 N.C.O. & 1 man proceeded to Boulogne as escort for Gnr Smith, Prisoner	
"	26			
"	27	- - -	One Man for Duty to 47th Brigade R.F.A.	
"	28	- - -	1 NCO " " " " " " " } Drill & Camp Fatigues	
"	29	- - -	" " " " " }	
"	30	- - -	" " " " " }	

Lt. RGA
Comdg X/14 T M Bty

2449 Wt. W14957/M90 750,000 1/16 J.B.C. & A. Forms/C.2118/12.

Army Form C. 2118.

Instructions regarding War Diaries and Intelligence Summaries are contained in F. S. Regs., Part II. and the Staff Manual respectively. Title Pages will be prepared in manuscript.

WAR DIARY
or
~~INTELLIGENCE SUMMARY~~ of Y. 14. Trench Mortar Battery.
(Erase heading not required.)
for. November. 1917.

Place	Date	Hour	Summary of Events and Information	Remarks and references to Appendices
WULVERGHEM.	Nov. 1.		Battery at work on Emplacement & Revetting trench leading to it.	
			Gr NOLAN to Hospital with Trench Fever.	
	" 3.		Inspection by D.T.M.O.	
	4.		Deepen Gun Position 2ft. Gr HALLAM. on Leave.	
	5-12.		Continuing work on Gun Position.	
	12.		Gr EASTWOOD sent to Hospital with Trench Fever.	
			Medium Team played R.A. H.Q. in Div: Competition Football. (Lost 1-0)	
	14.		Handed over to D.T.M.O. 5 Australian Div:	
	15-17.		Men at work on Salvage.	
	18.		Moved by Lorry from WULVERGHEM to WATOU.	
			Battery billetted in shed outside village.	
WATOU.				
	20.		Bdr Mc GANN & 9 men sent to PICKERING DUMP for duty.	
	21.		Work on Camp & cleaning guns.	
	22.		Pte LATCHAM. on Leave.	
	24.		2Lt CLARKE. attached to 46 Bde for duty.	
	27		9 Medium personnel attached to A/47 for work.	
	29.		Gr NOLAN wounded.	
	30.		Gr SHARP on Leave.	

M. Edwards. Lt.
O.C. Y. 14 T.M.B.
30/11/17.

2449 Wt. W14957/M90 750,000 1/16 J.B.C. & A. Forms/C.2118/12.

Instructions regarding War Diaries and Intelligence Summaries are contained in F. S. Regs., Part II. and the Staff Manual respectively. Title Pages will be prepared in manuscript.

Army Form C. 2118.

~~WAR DIARY~~ or INTELLIGENCE SUMMARY of Z.14.T.M.B.

(Erase heading not required.)

Sheet 1

Place	Date	Hour	Summary of Events and Information	Remarks and references to Appendices
	November			
WULVERGHEM				
"	1st		2/Lt Wilkinson posted from A47 Battery R.F.A. to Z14 Batty T.Ms, as second officer	
"	1st to 7th		Training - Gun drill	
"	2nd		Gunners Stewart and Rimmer posted to Z14 TMB.	
"	8th to 10th		Work on construction of 6" bed and salvage of timber for same	
"	11th		Gun. Whitelaw admitted to hospital	
"	12th to 14th		Salvage work on MESSINES RIDGE; Shells and shell cases	
"	13th		Gun. Whitelaw evacuated to C.C.S. and struck off strength of Z14.	
"	15		5th Australian Division took over command of 33rd Division front from noon 15th.	
"	15th to 17		Showing 5 Aust. Div. round trenches and gun positions and handing over all trench and area stores to them.	
"	16th		Working party supplied to D47. Batty. R.F.A.	
"	18th		Left WULVERGHEM and proceeded to WATOU by motor lorry; Lt. Scott & 2/Lt Ogilvie going on before as billeting party	

2449 Wt. W14957/M90 750,000 1/16 J.B.C. & A. Forms/C.2118/12.

Army Form C. 2118.

Instructions regarding War Diaries and Intelligence Summaries are contained in F. S. Regs., Part II. and the Staff Manual respectively. Title Pages will be prepared in manuscript.

WAR DIARY *or* ~~INTELLIGENCE~~ SUMMARY of Z.14.T.M.B.

(Erase heading not required.)

Sheet 2.

Place	Date	Hour	Summary of Events and Information	Remarks and references to Appendices
WATOU	23rd		Lt Scott and 2Lt Ogilvie proceeded to BRANDHOEK AREA to obtain billets	
"	24th		Moved to No 15 Camp BRANDHOEK AREA by Motor lorries.	
"	25th		Handed over two prisoners under detention to V14 TMB	
"	26th		Cleaning guns and stores	
"	27th		Supplied 3 men and 1 N.C.O. for duty with 47 Brigade RFA	
	28th		Two men proceed on leave 3 men + 1 NCO for duty with A47 battery RFA.	
	29		Working party as yesterday for A47	
	30		Working party as before.	

[signature] Lt
Z14TMB.

2449 Wt. W14957/M90 750,000 1/16 J.B.C. & A. Forms/C.2118/12.

Army Form C. 2118.

Instructions regarding War Diaries and Intelligence Summaries are contained in F. S. Regs., Part II. and the Staff Manual respectively. Title Pages will be prepared in manuscript.

V/14 HEAVY TRENCH MORTAR BATTERY. Date 17/1

WAR DIARY
or
~~INTELLIGENCE SUMMARY~~
(Erase heading not required.)

November 1917

Place	Date	Hour	Summary of Events and Information	Remarks and references to Appendices
28 T.10.d.0.4	1 to 13	nightly	working party on 9.45 H.T.M. position in progress at 0.34.d.5.6.	
	3		Capt J. THOMSON-EVANS R.F.A. returns from leave & assumes Command of Battery	
	14		3 9.45" H.T.M. emplacement under construction handed over to X/5A T.M. Bty on relief	
	16		2 9.45" Heavy Trench Mortars handed over to X/5A T M. Bty. working party of 1 officer & 20 men to D/47 Bde R.F.A. to withdraw guns from position.	
WATOU	18		Billets at T.10.d.0.4 vacated. Battery proceeds to billets at WATOU	
	19 to 23		Battery in rest in billets at WATOU.	
	24		Billets at WATOU vacated. Battery proceeds to billets at BRANDHOEK STATION. G.12.b.5.7 Sheet 28.	
	26		1 NCO & 15 men attached to 47th Bde. H.Q. RFA. for duty. 2/Lt E.F. MELLOR R.F.A. attached C/46 Bde RFA for duty.	

2449 Wt. W14957/M90 750,000 1/16 J.B.C. & A. Forms/C.2118/12.

Army Form C. 2118.

Instructions regarding War Diaries and Intelligence Summaries are contained in F. S. Regs., Part II. and the Staff Manual respectively. Title Pages will be prepared in manuscript.

V/14 HEAVY TRENCH MORTAR BATTERY. No. 17 Date 2

WAR DIARY
or
~~INTELLIGENCE~~ SUMMARY
(Erase heading not required.)

Place	Date	Hour	Summary of Events and Information	Remarks and references to Appendices
BRANDHOEK	27 to 30	daily	Party of 1 Sgt and 20 men attached A/47 Bde. RFA for duty.	

J Thomson-Evans. Capt RFA
Comdg V/14 Heavy T.M. Batty.

2449 Wt. W14957/M90 750,000 1/16 J.B.C. & A. Forms/C.2118/12.

Instructions regarding War Diaries and Intelligence Summaries are contained in F. S. Regs., Part II. and the Staff Manual respectively. Title Pages will be prepared in manuscript.

WAR DIARY
or
~~INTELLIGENCE SUMMARY~~

(Erase heading not required.)

Army Form C. 2118.

X 14 TMB

Place	Date	Hour	Summary of Events and Information	Remarks and references to Appendices
¼ Mile S.E. of —Vlamertinghe	Dec.r 1st	10 am	Court of Enquiry Re Gnr Smith J.C. absentee, summary of Evidence heard at D.A.C. ~~[illegible]~~	
			8 Men at Pickering Dump temporarily attached, Remainder on Camp Fatigues &c	
"	2		Do Do Fatigue party to A/47 Remainder on Camp Repairs &c.	
"	3		Do Do " " " " " " " "	
	4			
	5			
	6		" " " " " " "	
	7			
	8			
	9		Inspection anti Gas Appliances. " " "	
Vlamertinghe	10		Do Do Moved into Vlamertinghe	
"	11		" " " Fatigue Party to A/47 Remainder on improvements of Billets	
"	12		" " " " " " " " "	"
	13th to 31st		8 men withdrawn from PICKERING Dump and sent to Tunnelling Co.	
	14th		Inspection of guns rifles & revolvers	
	13th to 30th		Working party supplied daily to either 46th or 47 Brigade RFA except 25th & 26th	
	17		1 man goes on leave	
	18		1 Officer (Mr NORTHFIELD) goes on special leave, Court Martial Trial of Gunner Smith	
	19		Gunner Smith removed to detention camp BRANDHOEK.	

2449 Wt. W14957/M90 750,000 1/16 J.B.C. & A. Forms/C.2118/12.

Army Form C. 2118.

Instructions regarding War Diaries and Intelligence Summaries are contained in F. S. Regs., Part II. and the Staff Manual respectively. Title Pages will be prepared in manuscript.

WAR DIARY
or
~~INTELLIGENCE SUMMARY~~
(Erase heading not required.)

1 X 14 TMB

Place	Date	Hour	Summary of Events and Information	Remarks and references to Appendices
VLAMERTINGHE				
"	21st December		Inspection of guns, rifles & revolvers.	
"	24th		Inspection of antigas appliances	
"	25th		Christmas day, no working parties supplied, holiday observed	
"	26th		no working parties supplied inspection of billets	
"	27th		Working parties resumed with party to 46th Brigade R.F.A.	
	31st		Working party to D.A. All attached men returned to unit.	

G H Scott Lt
act OC X14TMB.

2449 Wt. W14957/M90 750,000 1/16 J.B.C. & A. Forms/C.2118/12.

Army Form C. 2118.

Instructions regarding War Diaries and Intelligence Summaries are contained in F. S. Regs., Part II. and the Staff Manual respectively. Title Pages will be prepared in manuscript.

WAR DIARY
or
~~INTELLIGENCE~~ SUMMARY

(Erase heading not required.)

Y/14 T.M.B.

Vol 21

Place	Date	Hour	Summary of Events and Information	Remarks and references to Appendices
BRADHOEK AREA	1st Dec.		9 O.Rs. attch. for duty. Pickering Dump.	
	2		Party at work on gun positions 46th Bde.	
	3.		Sgt. Walmsley killed	
	4.		" buried at Oxford Rd Cemetery.	
	5, 6, 7, 8		Working party as usual Inspection of gas appliance + rifle + revolvers.	
	9.		Gr. Boynton admitted to hospital from Dump.	
VLAMERTINGHE AREA	10		Moved to Vlamertinghe	
	11, 12		Working parties as usual.	
	13.		Lt. Edward on leave to England.	
	14.		usual.	
	15			
	16.		Gr. Sharp. returned from leave.	
	17.		Gr. Diamond. reported after avoiding escort from Havre.	
	18		usual working party inspection of gas masks. + battery stores.	
	19.		Bdr Allinson to hospital + Gr. Diamond remanded for C.M. Gr. Boynton discharged from hospital	
	20, 21		As usual	
	22.		Escort for Gr. Diamond's escort arrive + taken on ration strength pending C.M.	
	23		As usual.	
	24.		Gr. MacDonald. on leave.	
	25, 26, 27, 28		As usual. except 25 + 26 no working party required by 46 + 47 Bde.	
	29.		Gr. Diamond for C.M. Lt Edwards retd from leave	
	30.			
	31.		As usual.	

E.H. Wilkinson 2/Lt
Act O.C. Y/14 T.M.B.

2449 Wt. W14957/M90 750,000 1/16 J.B.C. & A. Forms/C.2118/12.

Army Form C. 2118.

Instructions regarding War Diaries and Intelligence Summaries are contained in F. S. Regs., Part II. and the Staff Manual respectively. Title Pages will be prepared in manuscript.

WAR DIARY
or
~~INTELLIGENCE~~ SUMMARY

(Erase heading not required.)

Z 14 TMB

Place	Date	Hour	Summary of Events and Information	Remarks and references to Appendices
BRANDHOEK AREA.	1st December		8 men attached for duty at PICKERING A.R.P.	
	2nd to 9th.		Daily party working for 46th Brigade R.F.A. on gun positions	
	6th		One man admitted to hospital (Gun Lath)	
	7th		One man evacuated from district + struck of strength of Z14.	
			One man ~~proceed~~ goes ~~for~~ on leave, Inspection of Rifles + revolvers + guns	
	9th		Inspection of gas appliances	
	10th		Moved from BRANDHOEK Area to VLAMERTINGHE.	
			One man goes on leave	
VLAMERTINGHE	11th + 12th		Party working for A47 on gun positions	
	13th to 31st		6 men withdrawn from ARP. and attached to Tunnelling Co.	
	14th		Inspection of guns, rifles + revolvers, 1 man returns from leave	
	15th		One man goes on leave	
	13th to 30th		Working parties daily except 25th an 26th for 46th + 47th Brigades	

2449 Wt. W14957/M90 750,000 1/16 J.B.C. & A. Forms/C.2118/12.

Army Form C. 2118.

Instructions regarding War Diaries and Intelligence Summaries are contained in F. S. Regs., Part II. and the Staff Manual respectively. Title Pages will be prepared in manuscript.

WAR DIARY
or
~~INTELLIGENCE SUMMARY~~
(Erase heading not required.)

Z14 TMB

Place	Date	Hour	Summary of Events and Information	Remarks and references to Appendices
VLAMERTINGHE				
	23rd December		One man goes on leave and one man returns from leave	
	25th		Christmas day, No parties supplied ~~to~~ Brigade & holiday observed	
	26th		No, parties required today.	
	27th		Work resumed this morning, Working party to 46th Brigade	
	31st		Men attached to PICKERING A.R.P. and Tunnelling Co. return to unit Working party to D.A.	

G H Scott Lt.
OC Z14 TMB

2449 Wt. W14957/M90 750,000 1/16 J.B.C. & A. Forms/C.2118/12.

Army Form C. 2118.

WAR DIARY
or
INTELLIGENCE SUMMARY
(Erase heading not required.)

Instructions regarding War Diaries and Intelligence Summaries are contained in F. S. Regs., Part II. and the Staff Manual respectively. Title Pages will be prepared in manuscript.

V/14 Hvy T M Bty
Dec 1917

Place	Date	Hour	Summary of Events and Information	Remarks and references to Appendices
BRANDHOEK	1 to 3	daily	Party of 1 N.C.O. and 16 men attached 47th Bde RFA for duty	
			" " 21 men attached F.A. Bdes. for duty	
	3		2/Lt E.F. MELLOR R.F.A. returns from C/46 to duty with Batty.	
	4 to 6		Party of 1 N.C.O. and 16 men attached 47th Bde R.F.A. for duty.	
			" " 21 men attached F.A. Bdes for duty.	
	6		2Lt J.P.F. OGILVIE attached C/46 Bde for duty.	
	7 to 10		Party of 1 N.C.O. and 16 men attached 47th Bde RFA for duty	
			" " 21 men attached F.A. Bdes for duty.	
VLAMERTINGHE. 28·H.3.c.2.0	10		Billets at BRANDHOEK vacated. Battery proceeds to Billets at VLAMERTINGHE	
	11 to 27		Party of 1 N.C.O. + 16 men attached 47th Bde RFA for duty	
			" " 21 men attached F.A. Bdes for duty.	
	27		2Lt E.F. MELLOR R.F.A. proceeds on leave to ENGLAND.	
	27 to 31		Party of 1 N.C.O. + 16 men attached 47th Bde RFA for duty	
			" " 21 men attached F.A. Bdes for duty.	

J. Thomson Evans Capt RFA
Comdg V/14 Heavy T.M. Batty.

2449 Wt. W14957/M90 750,000 1/16 J.B.C. & A. Forms/C.2118/12.

Original X/14 T M Bty

Army Form C. 2118.

Instructions regarding War Diaries and Intelligence Summaries are contained in F. S. Regs., Part II. and the Staff Manual respectively. Title pages will be prepared in manuscript.

WAR DIARY
or
INTELLIGENCE SUMMARY.

(Erase heading not required.)

Vol 22

Place	Date JANY	Hour	Summary of Events and Information	Remarks and references to Appendices
~~JANUARY~~ VLAMERTINGHE	1st		Rifle, Foot & 6" T.M. Drill & Preparations for Move.	
	2nd		Left VLAMERTINGHE arrived at Steenwoorde Billeted men & stayed the night	
	3rd		Left Steenwoorde for RENESCURE, arriving there at 3 P.M. Billeted men & stored guns & stores	
RENESCURE	4th		FOOT & RIFLE Drill cleaning Billets.	
" and	5th		Left RENESCURE for entraining point, St OMER. Entrained	
St Omer	6th		Left St OMER at 1.45 a.m. arrived at BUIRE at 11.30 a.m. detrained & proceeded to ETINEHAM arrived	6 P.M.
ETINEHAM	7th		BILLET IMPROVEMENTS, Foot, Rifle & T.M. Drill	
	8th 9th 10th 11th 12th 13th 14th 15th 16th 17th 18th		" "	
			" "	
"	19th		Left for 6" T.M. Course at VALEREAUX, marched to CORBIE, stayed there 1 night	
CORBIE	20		Left for VALEREAUX arriving there at 6 PM	
VALEREAUX	21st to 31st		At ~~6~~ T.M. 5th Army School of Instruction VALEREAUX.	

E.P. Northfield 2/Lt
for O.C. X/14 T.M.B.

A6945 Wt. W11422/M1160 350,000 12/16 D. D. & L. Forms/C./2118/14.

Original

Army Form C. 2118.

Instructions regarding War Diaries and Intelligence Summaries are contained in F. S. Regs., Part II. and the Staff Manual respectively. Title Pages will be prepared in manuscript.

WAR DIARY or ~~INTELLIGENCE SUMMARY~~ of Y. 14, Trench Mortar Battery. for January 1918.

(Erase heading not required.)

Place	Date	Hour	Summary of Events and Information	Remarks and references to Appendices
VLAMERTINGHE	Jan 1.		In camp at Vlamertinghe.	
	" 2.		Moved to Steenvoorde by Lorry.	
STEENVOORDE.	" 3.		Moved from Steenvoorde to Renescure by Lorry.	
RENESCURE	" 4.		In Billets at Renescure.	
	" 5		Entrained at St Omer. 5 O.R. with "Z" Battery leave for IV Army T.M. School.	
	" 6.		Arrived at Etinehem.	
ETINEHEM.	7 & 8.		Drill at Billets.	
	9.		Baths at Bray - change of Underclothing.	
			Bdr McGann goes on leave.	
	10-18.		Training at Etinehem.	
	19.		Return of 5 O.R. from T.M. School. Remainder leave for V Army T.M. School with "X".	
	20.		Cpl Illingworth goes on leave	
	21.		Gr Boynton " " "	
	22.		Inspection of Battery at 2" Drill - by Brig: Gen: Harding-Newman.	
	24.		Move from Etinehem to Sept Fours - by five Lorries.	
SEPT. FOURS.	25.		Moved from Sept. Fours to Guiscard.	
GUISCARD.	26.		D.T.M.O., Lt EDWARDS, & 2 O.R. take over Billets from French T. Mortars at Jussy.	
	27		Gun positions in trenches reconnoitred.	
	30.		Moved to Jussy.	

E.M. Edwards. Lt.
O.C. Y. 14 T.M.B.
30.1.18

2449 Wt. W14957/M90 750,000 1/16 J.B.C. & A. Forms/C.2118/12.

Instructions regarding War Diaries and Intelligence Summaries are contained in F. S. Regs., Part II. and the Staff Manual respectively. Title Pages will be prepared in manuscript.

Original

WAR DIARY
or
INTELLIGENCE SUMMARY
(Erase heading not required.)

Z 14 T.M.B.

Army Form C. 2118.

Place	Date	Hour	Summary of Events and Information	Remarks and references to Appendices
Vlamertinghe	Jan 1st		Kit Inspection.	
	2.		Moved to Steenvoorde by lorry.	
	3		" from " to Renescure.	
	4.		Inspection of mens equipment & kit.	
	5.		Entrained at St. Omer for 14th Army School.	
	6		"	
Vaux en Amienois	7		Arrived at School of Mortars Vaux.	
	7/19		Under instruction on 6" Newton Trench Mortar.	
	20		Entrained at Amiens for Etinehem.	
	21		Capt Hyde on leave.	
	22.		Inspection by Brig. Gen. of 14 Div. Art.	
	23		Testing of Box Respirators in gas chamber.	
	24		Moved to Sept Fours.	
Guiscard.	25.		Moved to Guiscard.	
	26.		Marching drill.	
	27.		Taken over Mortar position by French.	
	28		} Two parades daily.	
	29			
Jussy.	30		Moved to Jussy.	
	31.		Inspection of stores & billets.	

B Wilkinson 2/Lt
O/C. Z 14 T.M.B.

2449 Wt. W14957/M90 750,000 1/16 J.B.C. & A. Forms/C.2118/12.

Original

Army Form C. 2118.

WAR DIARY
or
~~INTELLIGENCE~~ SUMMARY
(Erase heading not required.)

Instructions regarding War Diaries and Intelligence Summaries are contained in F. S. Regs., Part II. and the Staff Manual respectively. Title Pages will be prepared in manuscript.

V/14 H.T.M. Bty. January 1918.

Place	Date	Hour	Summary of Events and Information	Remarks and references to Appendices
VLAMERTINGHE 28.H.3.c.2.0	1		Battery in Billets at VLAMERTINGHE. Working party of 1 NCO. & 6 men attached 47th Bde RFA return to Batty.	
	2		Battery vacates billet at VLAMERTINGHE & proceeds to STEENVOORDE.	
	3		Billets at STEENVOORDE vacated. Battery proceeds to RENNESCURE.	
	4		Battery in billets at RENNESCURE.	
	5		Battery vacates billets at RENNESCURE & proceeds to ST. OMER to entrain.	
	6		Battery detrains at BUIRE & proceeds to billets at ETINEHEM.	
	7 to 18		Battery in rest in billets at ETINEHEM.	
	12		LT J.P.F. OGILVIE R.F.A proceeds on 14 days leave to England.	
	14		LT E.F. MELLOR RFA. rejoins from leave.	
	19		Battery proceeds to V Army School of Mortars on Course of 9.45" H.T.M.	
	20 to 31		At V Army School of Mortars on Course.	
	23		LT J.P.F. OGILVIE RFA posted to 46th Bde RFA.	

[illegible] Captain
D.T.M.O. 14th Div.

2449 Wt. W14957/M90 750,000 1/16 J.B.C. & A. Forms/C.2118/12.

Instructions regarding War Diaries and Intelligence Summaries are contained in F. S. Regs., Part II. and the Staff Manual respectively. Title Pages will be prepared in manuscript.

WAR DIARY
or
INTELLIGENCE SUMMARY
(Erase heading not required.)

X/14 Trench Mortar Bty

Army Form C. 2118.

Feby. 1918.

Place	Date	Hour	Summary of Events and Information	Remarks and references to Appendices
Shutbbl [illegible] MISERY ; JUSSY	5/2/18		Battery reorganised under new Establishment. R G A personnel transferred to V/14 H T M Bty. 7 O R's transferred from V/14 H T M Bty. 2 O R's transferred from Z/14 T M Bty. Lieut Mellor R G A posted from V/14 H T M Bty	T M Bty
	7/2/18		2 officers & 12 O R's up the line digging suggested positions at ESSIGNY	
	11/2/18		6 6" T M's arrive from Ordnance	
	[illegible]/2/18		1 O R transferred from V/14 H T M Bty	
	[illegible]		Capt J Thomson Evans R F A from V/14 H T M Bty to be O. C. X/14 T M Bty	
	[illegible]/2/18		Remainder of battery on Gun Drill etc	
	21/2/18		Capt J Thomson Evans R F A on leave of absence Lt E T Mellor R G A assumes command of battery	
	[illegible]/2/18		2 officers 7 O R's on working party digging positions at URVILLERS, with party of 1 officer 12 O R's mentioned above 9. 2. 18 and 16 O R's from Y/14 T M Bty	
	2?/2/18		2 officers & 13 O R's to ESSIGNY building emplacements for 6" T M's	

E T Mellor
Lieut R G A
Comdg X/14 T M Bty

2449 Wt. W14957/M90 750,000 1/16 J.B.C. & A. Forms/C.2118/12.

Army Form C. 2118.

Instructions regarding War Diaries and Intelligence Summaries are contained in F. S. Regs., Part II. and the Staff Manual respectively. Title Pages will be prepared in manuscript.

WAR DIARY or INTELLIGENCE SUMMARY

V/14 Trench Mortar Bty

(Erase heading not required.)

Feby 1918

Vol 23

Place	Date	Hour	Summary of Events and Information	Remarks and references to Appendices
Sheet 66 C M15 B 04 JUSSY	1/2/18		5 O R's to Fifth Army School of Mortars on 6" T M Course.	
	3/2/18		Battery reorganised under new establishment. R G A Personnel transferred to V/14 H T M Bty. 22 OR's transferred from V/14 H T M Bty. 6 OR's transferred from X/14 T M Bty. 3 OR's transferred from X/14 T M Bty	
	5/2/18 to 10/2/18		Battery drill etc	
	11/2/18		Party of 1 officer & 25 OR's digging 4 gun positions in the line for battery. 6 6" T M's arrive from Ordnance	
	13/2/18		Lieut G H Scott R F A Ob late Z/14 T M Bty posted to battery	
	14/2/18 to 22/2/18		Reconnoitring positions, etc at ESSIGNY men on Gun drill etc	
	23/2/18		1 Bdr promoted Cpl. 3 Gnrs promoted Bdrs. 1 Bdr transferred to X/14 T M Bty 1 Gnr posted from X/14 T M Bty	
	23/2/18 to 26/2/18		Men at work on positions at ESSIGNY	
	27/2/18		Reconnoitring by URVILLERS	
	28/2/18		Commenced work on 6 Emplacements at URVILLERS	

E. M. Edwards. Capt
Comdg V/14 T M Bty

2449 Wt. W14957/M90 750,000 1/16 J.B.C. & A. Forms/C.2118/12.

6 14 DTM Bty 24 25 June & July

Army Form C. 2118.

WAR DIARY
or
~~INTELLIGENCE SUMMARY.~~
(Erase heading not required.)

Instructions regarding War Diaries and Intelligence Summaries are contained in F. S. Regs., Part II. and the Staff Manual respectively. Title pages will be prepared in manuscript.

Place	Date	Hour	Summary of Events and Information	Remarks and references to Appendices
MINDEN BARRACKS. DEEPCUT.	17 6/18		Formation of X & Y/14 "Newton" 6" Medium Trench Mortar Batteries. Personnel. X/14 Officers & Men: O/C. A/Capt Ruddy A.J., Lt. Tolputt H.St.G., 2nd Lt. Naylor J.W., " Pollitt C.E. — 53 O. Ranks. Y/14 Officers & Men: O/C. A/Capt Gimson A.F. (M.C.), Lt. Rendall F.G., 2nd Lt. Bryant L.A. — 46 O. Ranks.	
MINDEN BARRACKS. DEEPCUT.	4/7/18.	10 P.M.	Entrained Farnborough at 1 AM. for Folkestone.	
FOLKESTONE	5/7/18	8 AM.	Embarked for France.	
BOULOGNE	5/7/18	12 NOON	Disembarked Boulogne, & proceeded to Ostrohove Rest Camp Boulogne	
Ostrohove Rest Camp	6/7/18	8.30 AM.	Proceeded by Lorrie to 2nd Army Trench Mortar School, Leulinghem	
2nd Army Trench Mortar School.			Two weeks Course on 6" Medium Trench Mortars.	
"	17/7/18.		Capt Gimson A.F. appointed 14th Divisional Trench Mortar Officer with effect from 4/7/18.	
"	"		Lt. A/Capt Rendall F.G. takes over Command of Y/14 T.M.B vice Capt Gimson A.F. with effect from 5/7/18.	
"	20/7/18.		Proceeded to Rest Billets after Course at School, Helvelinghem (27A St Omer W15.16 Central)	
Helvelinghem	23/7/18 & 24/7/18.		Two Gunners to Base, & struck off Strength of X/14 Battery	
"	29/7/18.		Lt. Tolputt H.St.G. of X/14 & 1 Gunner of Y/14 Proceeded to RA Base Depot Havre auth; A.D.M.S. 14th Division.	
	30/7/18.		1 Cpl & 1 Gunner to Base & struck off Strength of X/14 Battery.	

A. F. Gimson. Capt. RGA
DTMO. 14th

D. D. & L., London, E.C.
(20346) W1 W5300/P713 750,000 3/18 E 2688 Forms/C/2118/16.

To "G" Office

14th Division Headquarters

Enclosed please find War Diary for

August period re XCY/14 T.M. Battery.

[illegible] Capt R.F.A.

D.T.M. Officer 14 Division

D.T.M.O.,
14TH DIVISION.

No. 151/H.

Date 12-9-18.

Instructions regarding War Diaries and Intelligence Summaries are contained in F. S. Regs., Part II. and the Staff Manual respectively. Title pages will be prepared in manuscript.

WAR DIARY or ~~INTELLIGENCE SUMMARY.~~

(Erase heading not required.)

Army Form C. 2118.

X/14 & Y/14 (M) Trench Mortar Batteries R.F.A.

Vol 26

Place	Date	Hour	Summary of Events and Information	Remarks and references to Appendices
Helvinghem	2/8/18	10.30AM	Both Batteries proceeded by Motor Lorries to St Sylvestre Capelle (Sheet 27 E&S P29.c.2.3) as a working Party digging Gun Positions	
			X/14 T.M Battery attached to 29th Durham Light Infantry for Rations.	
			Y/14 T.M Battery " " 14 Argyll & Sutherland Highlanders for Rations.	
St Sylvestre Capelle	12/8/18	8am	Both Batteries proceeded on foot to Steenvoorde Station, entrained their for St Mommlin, detrained St Mommlin & proceeded on foot to Rest Camp, Serques.	
Serques (Rest Camp)	13/8/18	8.30AM	Both Batteries Returned to Helvinghem by road, reaching same at 2P.M.	
Helvinghem	14/8/18	12 Noon	Lt Crompton. G. R.F.A. Posted to Y/14 T.M Battery from 14th D.A.C. with effect from 15/8/18	
"	15/8/18	9am	one Corporal evacuated to C.C. Station & struck off Y/14 T.M Battery R.F.A. with effect from 15/8/18	
"	17/8/18	1.30PM	one L/Bdr " " " " " X/14 T.M " " " " 17/8/18	
"	19/8/18	8.30AM	Batteries proceeded on foot to Autingues (Sheet Calais F.2.d.).	
Autingues	23/8/18	"	" " " " Northkerque Station, entrained their for Proven Station, detrained, & proceeded to Paradon Camp (Sheet 27 F.15.d.1.18).	
Proven (Paradon Camp)	26/8/18	9am	one Gunner of X/14 T.M.B transferred to Base for reclassification & struck off strength with effect from 27/8/18	
"	28/8/18	12 Noon	Batteries Marched to Border Camp (sheet 28/A 30 Central)	
Border Camp	29/8/18	9am	one Gunner evacuated to C.C. Station (X/14 T.M.B) & struck off strength with effect from 30/8/18	
"	31/8/18	7P.M.	Captain A.J. Ruddy O/c X/14 T.M Battery transferred to England & relinquishes Command of same (auth; A.G. 5999 (O) Sec Army A 305/1233 14th Divl d/4/9/18).	

A.T. [illegible] Capt RFA DTMO 14th Div

D. D. & L., London, E.C. (10340) Wt W3300/P713 750,000 3/18 E 2688 Forms C/2118/16.

Instructions regarding War Diaries and Intelligence Summaries are contained in F. S. Regs., Part II. and the Staff Manual respectively. Title pages will be prepared in manuscript.

WAR DIARY
or
~~INTELLIGENCE SUMMARY.~~
(Erase heading not required.)

Army Form C. 2118.

X & Y/14 Medium Trench Mortar Battery R.F.A.

Place	Date	Hour	Summary of Events and Information	Remarks and references to Appendices
Helringham	2 8/18	10.30 AM.	Both Batteries proceeded by Motor Lorries to St Sylvestre Capelle (Sheet 27 Ed 3. P.24.c.2.3.) as a working Party digging Gun Positions.	
			X/14 T.M. Battery attached to 29th Durham Light Infantry for Rations	
			Y/14 T.M. Battery " " 14th Argyll & Sutherland Highlanders for Rations	
St Sylvestre Capelle	12 8/18	8 AM.	Both Batteries proceeded on foot to Steenvorde Station, entrained there for St Momelin, detrained St Momelin & proceeded on foot to Rest Camp Serques.	
Serques. (Rest Camp)	13 8/18.	8.30 AM.	Both Batteries returned to Helringham by road reaching same at 2 P.M.	
Helringham	14 8/18.	12 Noon	Lt Crompton G. R.F.A. Posted to Y/14 T.M.B. from 14th D.A.C with effect from 15 8/18.	
"	15 8/18.	9 am	One Corporal evacuated to C.C. Station & struck off Strength of Y/14 T.M. Battery R.F.A. with effect from 15 8/18.	
"	17 8/18.	1.30 PM.	One L/Bdr " " " " " " " X/14 " " " " " 17 8/18.	
"	19 8/18.	8.30 AM.	Batteries proceeded on foot to Autingues (Sheet Calais F.2.d.)	
Autingues	23 8/18	"	" " " " " Nortkerque Station. Entrained there for Proven Station, detrained & proceeded to Poundon Camp (Sheet 27 F.15.d.1.8).	
Proven (Poundon Camp)	26 8/18	9 am	1 Gunner of X/14 T.M.B. transferred to Base for reclassification, & struck off strength with effect from 27 8/18.	
"	28 8/18	12 Noon.	Batteries marched to Border Camp (sheet 28/A.30 Central.)	
Border Camp.	29 8/18.	9 am	1 Gunner evacuated to C.C. Station (X/14 T.M. Battery) & struck off strength with effect from 30 8/18.	
"	31 8/18	7 P.M.	Capt A.J. Ruddy o/c of X/14 T.M. Battery transferred to England & relinquishes Command of same. (auth; A.G. 5999 (O) Sec Army. A.305/1233 14 Divl d/4 9/18).	

[illegible signature] Capt R.A. DTMO 14th Div

D. D. & L., London, E.C. (10340) Wt W4300/P713 750,000 3/18 E 2688 Forms/C/2118/16.

October 1918

Instructions regarding War Diaries and Intelligence Summaries are contained in F. S. Regs., Part II. and the Staff Manual respectively. Title pages will be prepared in manuscript.

WAR DIARY
or
~~INTELLIGENCE SUMMARY~~.
(Erase heading not required.)

Army Form C. 2118.

Vol 31

Place	Date	Hour	Summary of Events and Information	Remarks and references to Appendices
Ottowa Camp.	7/10/18	9am.	Battery moved to Eastwood Camp. (28T. 14 6.0.5.)	
Eastwood Camp.	4/10/18		General Fatigues at R.A. Hdqtr. Stc.	
	10/10/18		Party proceeded to captured Enemy 5.9 How. positions 0.28. C.7.3.	
	11/10/18	7am.	do. Fired 14 Rounds from Enemy 5.9 How. at above.	
	16/10/18	5.30 am.	Battery moved to Korentje (Sheet 28 T.26. C.9.4).	
	20/10/18	6am.	do. Tourcoing (Sheet 28. X29a. 6.7.)	
Korentje.	28/10/18	2pm.	3-0. Ranks proceeded to II Army Trench Mortar School for Course held on 29/10/18	
Tourcoing	28/10/18	5pm.	Battery moved to Trois Farms (Sheet 29. U.20.d 60.45).	
do.	29/10/18	9am.	Party of 1 Of. & 20. O. Ranks proceeded to prepare positions at U.29.C.2.4 for 9T. Mortars.	
Trois Farms.	30/10/18	4.30 am.	do. 5 O. Ranks do. do. do.	
do.	do.	5pm.		

Chas. Pollitt Lieut. R.F.A.
Comg. X/14 M. Trench Mortar Bty. R.F.A.

D. D. & L., London, E.C.
(10340) Wt W5300/P713 750,000 3/18 E 2688 Forms C/2118/16.

Instructions regarding War Diaries and Intelligence Summaries are contained in F. S. Regs., Part II. and the Staff Manual respectively. Title pages will be prepared in manuscript.

Army Form C. 2118.

WAR DIARY
or
INTELLIGENCE SUMMARY.
(Erase heading not required.)

X/41 Med Trench Mortar Bty RFA

Place	Date	Hour	Summary of Events and Information	Remarks and references to Appendices
Ottawa Camp 28/G.24.c.6.5	30/9/18	16.00	1 Officer (Lieut Crompton L) + 1 other Rank proceeded on "Course" to 2nd Army Trench Mortar School	
"	2/10/18	4.69	Moved to Eastwood Camp 28/I.14.b.0.5	
"	4/10/18 to 10/10/18		General Fatigues at RA Headquarters 41st Division	
"	3/10/18	08.00	1 Sergt (B Sub Clerk att X/41) posted to RA Headquarters 62nd Division	
"	11/10/18	11.59	3 Corporals + 2 Gunners reported from 41st DAC	
"	12/10/18	08.00	1 Officer (Capt Rundall O/C X/41) to Hospital (Sick) 14th CCS. Lieut Bryant LA taking over Command of Battery	
"	13/10/18	14.00	1 Corporal (B Sub Clerk att X/41) reported from A/41 Bde RFA	
"	14/10/18	"	1 Gunner reported from 41st DAC	
"	"	1159	1 Corporal posted to 4/41st Army Brigade RFA	
"	15/10/18	18.00	1 Gunner reported from C/41 Bde RFA	
"	17/10/18	11.00	1 Officer (2/Lt Stringer C.W.) reported from B/41 Bde RFA	
"	19/10/18	18.00	Moved to Rorentje (28/J.28.c.9.7)	
"	21/10/18	14.00	Moved to Tourcoing (28/X.29.a.6.7)	
Rorentje 28/J.28.c.9.7			1 Corporal reported from 7/41st Army Brigade RFA	
Tourcoing 28/X.29.a.6.7	23/10/18	14.00		
	24/10/18	15.00	1 Officer (Lieut Crompton L) + 1 other Rank reported from "Course" at 2nd Army TM School (Lieut Crompton taking over Command of Battery	
"	25/10/18	14.00	1 Gunner posted to X/41	
"	26/10/18	12.00	2 Officers + 20 other ranks proceeded up line to take up positions (3 Guns + 80 CAS) at 37/G.9.c.16.20	
"	28/10/18	14.00	1 Officer (2/Lt Stringer C.W.) + 6 other ranks proceeded on Course at 2nd Army TM School	
"	29/10/18	10.30	Moved to Trois Farm 37/U.2.d. cent	

(10342) Wt W5500/P713 750,000 5/18 E 2688 D. D. & L., London, E.C. Forms C/2118/18.

Instructions regarding War Diaries and Intelligence Summaries are contained in F. S. Regs., Part II. and the Staff Manual respectively. Title pages will be prepared in manuscript.

WAR DIARY
or
INTELLIGENCE SUMMARY.
(Erase heading not required.)

Army Form C. 2118.

Y/Med Trench Mortar Bty. R.F.A.

Place	Date	Hour	Summary of Events and Information	Remarks and references to Appendices
Frow Farm 37/U. 20. d. cent	30/10/18	04.30	A party of 4 Other Ranks proceeded up line digging gun positions at 37/U. 29. c. 2. 4	
"	31/10/18	17.00	1 Officer (Lieut Crompton G) proceeded to UK on leave, Lieut Bryant taking over Command of Battery.	
"	"	17.00	4 Other Ranks proceeded up line digging gun positions at 37/U. 29. c. 2. 4	

A. F. Gunson Capt. R.F.A.
Comdg. Y/Med T.M.B.

D. D. & L., London, E.C.
(10349) Wt W5300/P713 750,000 3/18 E 2688 Forms C/2118/15.

Instructions regarding War Diaries and Intelligence Summaries are contained in F. S. Regs., Part II. and the Staff Manual respectively. Title pages will be prepared in manuscript.

Army Form C. 2118.

WAR DIARY or INTELLIGENCE SUMMARY.

(Erase heading not required.)

14th Div Trench Mortars (X & Y Bttys)

32 P. 12. 18

Place	Date	Hour	Summary of Events and Information	Remarks and references to Appendices
Trois Farm COYGHEM. 29/U 20a	1/11/18		1 Off. & 7 OR's of Y Bty to 29/C 9 c 15.20 to withdraw guns to Rest Billets (Trois Farm)	
			Remainder of Y Bty and X Bty on Fatigues, Physical Training etc.	
	2/11/18	20.30	Party of X Bty to positions 29/U 29 c 2.4. Fired 135 rds from 9 mortars on enemy positions 29/C 5 b 4.5	
			Remainder of X Bty and Y Bty on fatigues & P. T. Training	
	3/11/18.	04.05	Fired on Enemy positions 29/C 5 b 8.5 - 2.0. (X Bty)	
		19.30 to 22.45	" 50 rds " " 29/C 5 a 8.5 - 4.5. (do)	
			Remainder of Bttys on fatigues etc. Gas Helmet inspection (Y Bty)	
	4/11/18	23.20 to 24.00	X Bty fired 50 rds on Enemy positions 29/U 30 c.	
			" " 108 " " Road 29/C 6 a 4.4 - C 6 a 2.8	
			P. Training carried on by OR's at Rest Billet.	
	5/11/18		Heavy enemy shelling in vicinity of Rest billets (Yellow Cross) P.T continues	
	6/11/18.		1 O 6 R's of Y Bty and party of X Bty at 29/U 29 c 2.4. relieved Y Bty relieved X Bty at 37/U 28 a 90.60	
	8-10/11/18		Y Bty in the line. X Bty P. T and fatigues at Rest Billet.	
	11/11/18	11.00	notification received of Armistice.	
			8 mortars & accessories (immobile) (X & Y Bttys) handed in to Gun Park no 2.	
	12/11/18		all personnel of both Bttys in the line return to Rest billet	
	14/11/18.		Both Bttys and D T M O move from Trois Farm to WATTRELOS. 37/A 17 c 3. 1.	

D. D. & L., London, E.C.
(10340) W: W3300/P713 750,000 3/18 E 2688 Forms/C/2118/16.

Instructions regarding War Diaries and Intelligence Summaries are contained in F. S. Regs., Part II. and the Staff Manual respectively. Title pages will be prepared in manuscript.

Army Form C. 2118.

WAR DIARY
INTELLIGENCE SUMMARY.

14 Div Trench Mortars (X & Y Btties)

(Erase heading not required.)

1. 12. 18.

Place	Date	Hour	Summary of Events and Information	Remarks and references to Appendices
WATTRELOS 37/a17c31.	14/11/18	(cont)	Alteration in working of T.M. Btties. Only 2 6" T.M.'s mobile per Bty. Transport attached from 14 DAC viz:- 16 Drvs, 32 mules & 4 L.G.S. Waggons	
	15-17		General fatigues etc	
	18/11/18		Lt G. Crompton returned from leave and assumed command of Y Bty vice Lt. Bryant.	
	19/11/18		2 OR's of each Bty attached 15th N. Lancs Regt for agricultural work.	
	20/11/18		Lt W. M. Pratt posted to X Bty from X/41 T.M. Bty.	
			" transferred from X to Y Bty and takes over command of last named Bty vice Lt G. Crompton.	
	23/11/18		2/Lt C. W. Stringer and 9 OR's from attachment at Second Army School of mortars.	
			2/Lt D Eckersall takes over command of X Bty from Lt C.G. Pollett	
	24/11/18		One gunner Y Bty to Hospital Sick 1 Cpl Y Bty Leave to U.K. ~~etc~~	
	25/11/18		2 OR's X Bty leave to U.K.	
			Lt W M Pratt do (Y Bty) Lt G. Crompton takes over command Y Bty vice Lt Pratt	
	26/11/18 to 30/11/18		Physical Training, fatigues etc.	

A H Ginson Capt R.F.A.
DT.M.O 14 Div
Comdg. 14th Div T.M's (?)

D. D. & L., London, E.C.
(10340) Wt W5300/P713 750,000 5/18 E 2688 Forms/C/2118/16.

Instructions regarding War Diaries and Intelligence Summaries are contained in F. S. Regs., Part II. and the Staff Manual respectively. Title pages will be prepared in manuscript.

WAR DIARY
or
~~INTELLIGENCE SUMMARY.~~
(Erase heading not required.)

X/14-M. TRENCH
No. December 1918.
MORTAR BATTERY R.F.A.

Army Form C. 2118.

Vol 33

Place	Date	Hour	Summary of Events and Information	Remarks and references to Appendices
Wattrelos.	Dec 1	9am	One officer posted from Y/14 M. Trench Mortar Battery. R.F.A. + taken on Strength from + including that date.	
do	" 4	10am	Battery moved from 37/A.17.c.3.1. to 37/A.22.a.7.8.	
	" 11	10am	3 N.C.Os reinforcements arrive from D.A.C.	
	12		1 O.R. evacuated to C.C.S.	
	13		1 O.R. evacuated to C.C.S.	
	14		1 O.R. Coalminer despatched to Dispersal Camp	
	16		1 O.R. Transferred to Y/14 Med T.M. Bty	
	17		1 L/Bdr reverts to permanent rank of Gunner at own request.	
	19		2 O.R. despatched to Dispersal Camp	
	24		1 O.R. transferred to Y/14 M.T.M. Bty	
			2 O.R. — do — from Y/14 — do —	
			1 Cpl appointed a/Sgt.	
	28		1 O.R. admitted to Hospital	
	30		4 O.R attached to 1st Army T.M. School	
			1 O.R despatched to Dispersal Camp	
	31		Guard of 4 O.R. over Ammunition in forward area Bois Jacquet relieved.	

[signature]
Capt. R.G.A.
X/14 Med Trench Mortar Bty R.F.A

D. D. & L., London, E.C.
(10340) Wt W3300/P713 750,000 3/18 E 2688 Forms C/2118/16.

Instructions regarding War Diaries and Intelligence Summaries are contained in F. S. Regs., Part II. and the Staff Manual respectively. Title pages will be prepared in manuscript.

WAR DIARY
or
INTELLIGENCE SUMMARY.
(*Erase heading not required.*)

Army Form C. 2118.

Y/14 Med. Trench Mortar Bty R.F.A.

Place	Date	Hour	Summary of Events and Information	Remarks and references to Appendices
Wattrelos	2.11.18		2/Lt C.W. Stringer posted to X/14 T.M.B.	
37/I.17.C.3.1	4.12.18		Battery moved to Wattrelos 37/I.22.a.7.8	
37/I.22.a.7.8	5.12.18		One Bombardier on leave to UK.	
			One Gunner evacuated to CCS.	
	7.12.18		One Corporal posted from CA Reinforcements Depot	
			One Driver (att Y/14) evacuated to CCS.	
	13.12.18		One Corporal reported from leave.	
	"		One Gunner & one Dvr (att Y/14) to Dispersal Camp for Demobilization	
	14.12.18		Lieut Lom Pratt appointed A/Capt from 20/11/18 whilst Commanding Y/14 T.M.B.	
	"		Lieut Crompton G. appointed A/Capt from 15/10/18 to 20/11/18	
	"		Capt Lom Pratt & one Gunner reported from leave, Capt Lom Pratt	
	"		Assuming Command of Battery	
	"		One Driver (att Y/14 TMB) to Dispersal Camp for Demobilization	
	15.12.18		One Gunner posted to X/14 TMB.	
	"		One " from X/14 "	
	"		One Corporal promoted to Sergeant vice Sgt Broggan to hospital	
	"		Two Bombardiers " " Corporals " Cpl to Sergeant & one Corporal	
	"		to hospital sick	
	"		Three Drivers posted from 103 Sec 14 DAC	
	"		One Driver (att Y/14) on Course to 354 Crml Coy RE Concq	
	16.12.18		One Corporal (att Y/14), 3 gunners on leave to UK	
	"		Lieut Crompton G. & one Gunner (as batman) on Course to Institute of Chemistry, Rue Barthelemy Delespaul, Lille	
	"		Two gunners to Dispersal Camp for Demobilization	
	18.12.18		Capt A.J. Simpson (DSO MC) on leave to UK.	
	19.12.18		One Dvr (att Y/14) reported from course at 354 Crml Coy RE Concq	
	"		One Gunner (att 15th L.H.) evacuated to CCS.	

D. D. & L., London, E.C. (10340) Wt W3300/P713 750,000 3/18 E 2688 Forms/C/2118/16.

Instructions regarding War Diaries and Intelligence Summaries are contained in F. S. Regs., Part II. and the Staff Manual respectively. Title pages will be prepared in manuscript.

WAR DIARY
or
INTELLIGENCE SUMMARY.
(Erase heading not required.)

Army Form C. 2118.

Place	Date	Hour	Summary of Events and Information	Remarks and references to Appendices
[illegible]	22.12.18		Battery on Fatigues for Div Hdqrs at [illegible]	
7/1 A. M. a. f. [illegible]			One Gunner awarded 14 days F.P.	
	24.12.18		One Corporal & one Bombardier posted [illegible]	
			One Bombardier posted from [illegible]	
	"		One " Reported from leave.	
			One Corporal to Dispersal Camp for Demobilisation	
	28.12.18		Four other ranks on course to 1st Army T.M. School. [illegible]	
	29.12.18		One Corporal (D. Furman) to O/C Transfer Centre Eastern Command	
	31.12.18		[illegible]	
			One A/Bom promoted Bombardier	
			One Corporal 7 other ranks on Fatigues to 11 Ordnance Ammunition Section [illegible]	
			One Gunner to 1st Army Hdqrs.	
			One " Reported from Leave.	

[signature] Capt.

D. D. & L., London, E.C.
(10340) Wt W3500/P713 750,000 3/18 E 2688 Forms C/2118/14.

January 1919

Instructions regarding War Diaries and Intelligence Summaries are contained in F. S. Regs., Part II. and the Staff Manual respectively. Title pages will be prepared in manuscript.

WAR DIARY
or
INTELLIGENCE SUMMARY.
(Erase heading not required.)

X/14-M. TRENCH
No. 9570
MORTAR BATTERY R.F.A.

Army Form C. 2118.

Place	Date	Hour	Summary of Events and Information	Remarks and references to Appendices
Wattrelos	1/1/19		7 O/R attached No 11 Ord Ann Sec. Courtrai.	
	2/1/19		1 O/R " 14th D.A. H.Q.	
			1 O/R Demobilyzed.	
			1 O/R awarded 8 days C.B. & 3 Extra Guards for being absent from Guard 6.30 pm to 9.45 pm 28/12/18	
	4/1/19		1 O/R Demobilyzed	
	5/1/19		1 O/R —"—	
	6/1/19		1 O/R —"—	
	9/1/19		1914-15 Star Ribbon distributed to Officers. NCOs & Men entitled	
	11/1/19		2 O/R Demobilyzed	
	12/1/19		1 O/R —"—	
	13/1/19		2 Gnrs posted to Battery from 5th Army Reinforcement Camp	
			4 O/R return from Course at 1st Army Trench Mortar School	
	14/1/19		10 attached Drivers returned to 14th D.A.C.	
	17/1/19		2 remaining attd Drs " " "	
	18/1/19		1 O/R Demobilyzed.	
	20/1/19		2 O/R —"—	
	21/1/19		Capt Ecclesall D. O/C X/14 T.M. Bty & Lieut Pollett C.G. Demobilyzed.	
	22/1/19		4 O/R Demobilyzed	
			X & Y/14 T.M. Btys combined for Messing, Parades & Discipline under O/C Y/14 Bty	
	27/1/19		4 O/R Demobilyzed.	
	28/1/19		4 O/R —"—	
	29/1/19		4 O/R —"—	
			11 O/R Posted to No 1 Sec 14th DAC. 1 O/R to No 3 Sec 14th DAC 2 O/R to HQ 14th DAC.	

[signature]
Capt R.F.A.
X/14 Med Trench Mortar Bty RFA

D. D. & L., London, E.C.
(10340) Wt W5300/P713 750,000 3/18 E 2688 Forms/C/2118/16.

January 1919.

Instructions regarding War Diaries and Intelligence Summaries are contained in F. S. Regs., Part II. and the Staff Manual respectively. Title pages will be prepared in manuscript.

WAR DIARY
or
~~INTELLIGENCE SUMMARY.~~

(Erase heading not required.)

Y/14 M. TRENCH
No. 9/571
MORTAR BATTERY R.F.A.

14

Army Form C. 2118.

V8 34

Place	Date	Hour	Summary of Events and Information	Remarks and references to Appendices
Wattrelos	6/1/19		1 Officer 1 O/R rejoined Battery from Leave.	
	9/1/19		1914-15 Star Ribbon distributed to Officers NCOs & Men entitled to wear such.	
	11/1/19		1 O/R (attached) admitted to Hospital.	
	14/1/19		1 Cpl reported from 5th Army Reinforcement Camp	
			2 NCOs & 2 Men returned from Course at 1st Army School of Mortars.	
			2 O/R reported for duty from Hospital.	
			1 O/R demobilized.	
	15/1/19		9 Drivers attached from 14th D.A.C returned to their Sections	
	20/1/19		1 Cpl reported for duty from Hospital.	
			2 NCOs 1 man demobilized.	
	22/1/19		4. O/R demobilized	
	23/1/19		3. O/R — " —	
	25/1/19		2 O/R — " —	
	26/1/19		1 O/R Demobilized	
			1 Officer reported for duty from Course at No 2 G.H.Q. Chemistry School at Lille.	
	27/1/19		7. O/R demobilized.	
	28/1/19		5. O/R — " —	
	29/1/19		2 Officers 3 O/R Demobilized.	
			9 O/R posted to No 2 Section 14th D.A.C.	
			3 O/R " " No 3 " "	

[signature]
Capt R.F.A.
Y/14 Med Trench Mortar Bty RFA

D. D. & L., London, E.C.
(10340) W: W3300/P713 750,000 3/18 E 2688 Forms/C/2118/16.

www.ingramcontent.com/pod-product-compliance
Lightning Source LLC
Chambersburg PA
CBHW081403160426
43193CB00013B/2093

* 9 7 8 1 4 7 4 5 0 8 7 1 1 *